Scottish Archaeolo

Volume 26 parts 1 + 2 (2004)

'There is a castle in the west ...'

Dundonald Castle Excavations 1986–93

Gordon Ewart and Denys Pringle

with contributions by
David Caldwell, Ewan Campbell, Stephen Driscoll, Katherine Forsyth,
Dennis Gallagher, Tim Holden, Fraser Hunter, David Sanderson
and Jennifer Thoms

Published by
EDINBURGH UNIVERSITY PRESS LTD
on behalf of
THE GLASGOW ARCHAEOLOGICAL SOCIETY

The Journal is published with the financial support of
the Dalrymple Fund

Contents

Abstract

Three main seasons of archaeological excavation were completed at Castle Hill, Dundonald, Ayrshire between 1986 and 1988, in advance of a programme of conservation. Subsequently a series of smaller-scale excavations were undertaken until the final season in 1993. Six periods of settlement were identified in the excavated evidence, beginning with fortifications from the the transition from prehistory to the Early Historic period through to a series of increasingly complex castles built by the Stewarts. Remains were found of what was probably a 12th-century motte-and-bailey castle with a timber hall. This was succeeded by an elaborate 13th-century castle of enclosure with opposing gatehouses. This was in turn replaced by the late 14th-century castle of King Robert II, with its massive tower-house and enclosure wall or barmkin.

Contributors

Gordon Ewart, Kirkdale Archaeology, 4 Western Terrace, Edinburgh EH12 5QF

Professor Denys Pringle, Cardiff School of History and Archaeology, Cardiff University, Cardiff CF10 3EU

Dr David Caldwell, Royal Museums of Scotland, Chambers Street, Edinburgh EH1 1JF

Dr Ewan Campbell, Archaeology Department, University of Glasgow G12 8QQ

Professor Stephen T. Driscoll, Archaeology Department, University of Glasgow G12 8QQ

Dr Katherine Forsyth, Department of Celtic, University of Glasgow G12 8QQ

Dennis Gallagher, 4 Sylvan Place, Edinburgh EH9 1LH

Dr Tim Holden, Headland Archaeology Ltd, 13 Jane Street, Edinburgh EH6 5HE

Dr Fraser Hunter, Royal Museums of Scotland, Chambers Street, Edinburgh EH1 1JF

Dr David Sanderson, Scottish Univerities Research and Reactor Centre, East Kilbride G75 0QF

Jennifer Thoms, 11 Albert Street, Kirkwall, Orkney KW15 1HP

List of Figures

Preface and Acknowledgements

Dundonald Castle, the Ayrshire country retreat of the Scottish kings Robert II and Robert III, was finally abandoned as a residence towards the end of the 16th century. In 1638, it passed into the ownership of William Cochrane of Cowdon, who was created 1st Earl Dundonald by Charles II in 1669. In 1953 the 13th earl placed the site and its imposing ruins in the care of the state. Historic Scotland's predecessor bodies undertook a programme of masonry repair and conservation from the 1960s, the work being completed 1985–95. In 1986–8 and 1993 the masons working on the castle were joined by a team of archaeologists, directed by Gordon Ewart, who undertook a parallel programme of ground clearance and excavation. The Friends of Dundonald took over visitor management, having built an impressive visitor centre which opened in 1997. Historic Scotland retains responsibility for conservation of the fabric.

This volume represents the final definitive report on the archaeological work carried out at Dundonald during conservation of the ruins between 1986 and 1993. In writing it, Gordon Ewart took responsibility for drafting the sections relating to the below-ground archaeology, while Denys Pringle, who oversaw the project for Historic Scotland in 1990–3, has contributed the sections relating to the standing remains. In Section 3, we have attempted to combine our respective contributions into a single narrative, describing the structural development of the site over three millennia. In discussing the historical context and sources relating to Dundonald (Sections 2 and 6) we also gratefully acknowledge the valuable assistance of Dr William McQueen. His thoughts on the overall development of the site through his unpublished paper on 'The Stewarts and Dundonald' as well as on more specific areas of archival research concerning Dundonald (particularly Periods 5 and 7) have all informed much of our thinking about the castle.

We would also like to express our thanks to all those specialists who contributed to this report: David Caldwell, Ewan Campbell, Trevor Cowie, Stephen Driscoll, Julie Franklin, Fraser Hunter, Tim Holden, Nicholas Holmes, Nigel Ruckley, Robin Murdoch, Dennis Gallagher, Jennifer Thoms, Nicola Murray, Richard Grove, AOC Scotland Ltd, David Sanderson and Kurt Strickertson. Additional historical research was undertaken by Alex Gibson. Further expert guidance and support was provided by Chris Tabraham, the late Julian Small, John Hume and Peter Yeoman of Historic Scotland, as well as by Geoffrey Stell of the Royal Commission on the Ancient and Historical Monuments of Scotland.

The illustrations were drawn by Marion O'Neil (finds and pottery), David Connolly (plans and sections), David Simon (reconstructions) and Howard Mason (comparartive castle plans). The RCAHMS survey was carried out by John Borland and Douglas Boyd. The assistance of Joel Spencer and Andrew Douglas (SURRC) with TL sample preparation and measurements is gratefully acknowledged.

Editing, formatting and general organisation of the text and illustrations were completed by Andrew Dunn, Dennis Gallagher and Andrew Hollinrake.

Many individuals participated in the excavations, but special mention should go to Jon Triscott, David Stewart, John Lewis, Eion Cox, James Falconer, Alan Radley, Bob Will, Fiona Baker, Graham Wilson and Hazel Moore.

Special thanks also go to the following for their support and encouragement: Mr J. Stein of Millers Special Projects, Mrs Annie Steele and the Dundonald Masons (Charlie, Phil, and others) led by Sandy Alexander. Finally, the archaeological team wish to acknowledge the assistance of the numerous residents of Dundonald, whose support and interest proved invaluable to the success of the project.

The archaeological work at Dundonald was sponsored throughout by Historic Scotland, who have also contributed to the cost of this publication.

Gordon Ewart, Kirkdale Archaeology, Edinburgh.
Denys Pringle, Cardiff School of History and Archaeology, Cardiff University, Cardiff.

1 Site Location and Topography

The ruins of Dundonald Castle (NS 364 345) overlook the picturesque village of Dundonald in North Ayrshire, 13km (eight miles) west of Kilmarnock and the same distance south of Irvine (Figs 1 and 2).

The Castle Hill, on which the remains stand, is part of a ridge of low hills fringing the coastal plain, many of whose summits – as at Dundonald – have sustained settlement over many centuries. Castle Hill at Dundonald forms the northern limit of this rocky ridge, where it meets the flat expanse of Shewalton Moss. It commands panoramic views to the east and for some 30km northward over the north Ayrshire plain. To the west, the coastline, including the medieval castle sites of Ardrossan, Irvine and Portencross, is plainly visible, framed by the isle of Arran and the Paps of Jura beyond.

Despite medieval landscaping, the general contours of the natural hill are still largely discernible. It is likely that the earliest settlement of Dundonald, between the 1st millennium BC and the 1st millennium AD (Periods 1 and 2), was constrained in extent by the natural limits of the hill and most specifically by the nature of the parent rock itself. Geologically, the hill comprises a quartz-dolerite sill with limited till cover, well jointed and craggy in parts, and with a very obvious alignment north-east to south-west. By extrapolating the limits and heights of the bedrock in the excavated areas and by discounting areas of later landscaping, it is possible to gain a good impression of the area available for settlement in antiquity. The sharply shelving nature of the rock and its oblique alignment to the later, medieval layout (east–west) demonstrate how the highest point of the hill lent itself physically to some form of inner defensive line, fragments of which were revealed during the excavation. Areas of natural terracing similarly delineate the early line of outer defences, elements of which were also found.

The excavations have shed most light on the nucleus of this hillfort or dun, which as a discrete entity might be regarded as the 'citadel' of the larger complex. The latter certainly spread beyond these limits to the east and north.

Although much of the medieval fortification of the 11th and 12th centuries (Period 3) was obscured by the radical rebuilding on the site in the 13th century (Period 4), it is probable that its shape and point of access were determined to a large extent by the form and limits of the Period 2 fort. The site therefore demonstrates a notable continuity of occupation from prehistoric and early historic times through to the medieval period.

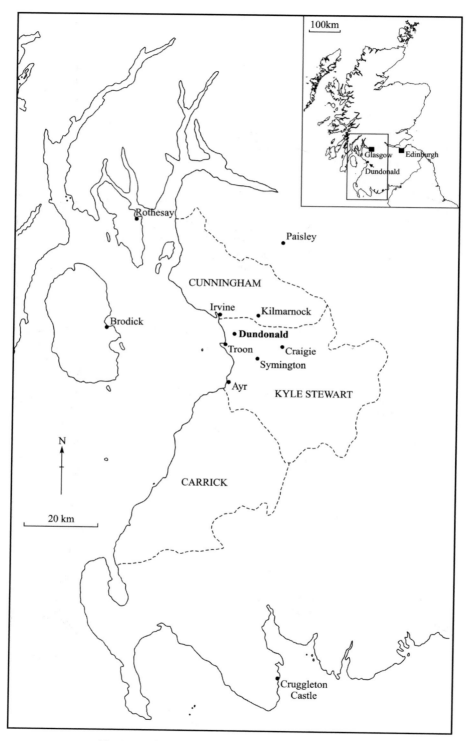

Fig 1 Dundonald Castle and the regions of Ayrshire.

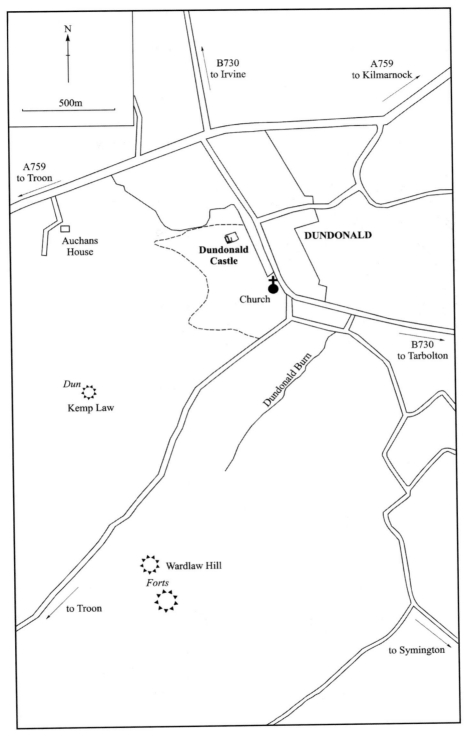

Fig 2 Local setting and road network around Dundonald.

2 Historical Background

THE LATE IRON AGE AND EARLY HISTORIC PERIOD

by Stephen Driscoll and Katherine Forsyth

Dundonald occupies a low-lying but prominent craggy hill, 4km inland from Troon with its natural harbour and a further 7km from the mouth of the River Irvine. In its physical characteristics and historical associations, Dundonald corresponds to major royal sites in northern Britain such as Dumbarton Rock, Edinburgh and Dunadd. On topographical grounds and archaeological evidence, Dundonald appears to be a regional power centre of the Early Historic period, but as the excavations show the site was occupied from the Bronze Age (Fig 3).

According to the 2nd-century Ptolemy of Alexandria the native Celtic peoples who occupied west central Scotland were called the *Damnonii* (Barrow 1989, Rivet and Smith 1979, Watson 1926, 15, 26). The early importance of the Dundonald area is reflected in Ptolemy's naming of *Vindogara Sinus*, 'Vindogara Bay' (Breeze 2002). The precise location of *Vindogara*, and whether it was a Roman or native site, cannot be established from classical sources. However, if Andrew Breeze (2002) is correct to interpret the name as meaning 'white shank/headland/ridge', then the sandy headland of Troon (from British, cf. Welsh *Trwyn* 'the nose, headland', Watson 1926, 191) is a likely site. Ptolemy, who is thought to have been drawing upon Roman military maps of the late 1st century AD, provides some insight into the Iron Age political geography of the region. *Vindogara* is one of six *poleis* ('cities') of the *Damnonii*; this large number of named centres (although mostly unidentified) implies a reasonable degree of social organisation. However, unlike their neighbours – to the east, the *Uotadini* (>Gododdin), and to the south, the *Novantae* (>Nouant) – the name of the *Damnonii* does not appear to have survived into the Early Historic period, at least not referring to a political unit. It may however be preserved in the placenames Car<u>dowan</u>, Wishaw, Lanarkshire (<British *caer* 'fort') and <u>Dowan</u>hill, Milngavie, Dunbartonshire (Wilkinson 2002, 143), which give important clues as to the extent of Damnonian territory, described by Barrow as 'the easily traversed territory from Kyle to the Lennox taking in Ayr, Irvine, Glasgow and Dumbarton'(1989, 162).

In the Early Historic period the area is referred to as *Aeron*. This river name, which survives today as Ayr, derives from Celtic *Agrona* 'goddess of slaughter' (Watson 1926, 342). *Aeron* is mentioned in several different contexts in Early British poetry: five times in the *Gododdin* corpus and in three early poems in the *Book of Taliesin* (VII.12, VIII.22, XI.21–2). There are of course substantial problems with heroic poetry for historical purposes, not least in explaining how poetry purporting to have been composed in the North during the 6th and 7th centuries came to be preserved in medieval Welsh manuscripts. These complex

Fig 3 Aerial photograph of the site from the east prior to recent conservation work (AP 1984: Neg. no. A65297: title NS 33 SE 2 – NS36363451, © Crown copyright, reproduced courtesy of RCAHMS).

questions of historical and linguistic context are fully discussed in John Koch's critical edition of the *Gododdin* (1997), while the early British poetry itself is readily accessible in translation through *The Triumph Tree* anthology (Clancy 1998). The *Gododdin* collection is widely perceived of as having an eastern focus, since it celebrates the heroes gathered by the lord of Din Eidyn (Edinburgh) to do battle at Catraeth (Yorkshire). Given that the geographical theatre of action is east of the Pennines, the prominence of Aeron seems decidedly out of place. Koch (1997, lxxx–lxxxiii) and most other modern scholars believe that this is because the cycle of poems that was transmitted to Wales came via Strathclyde where emphasis was given to figures with local resonance.

Aeron is mentioned in three of the late 6th-century poems found in the *Book of Taliesin* (Williams 1968), twice in connection with Urien of Rheged, who is described as the 'defender of Aeron' (VIII.22), presumably as its overlord. The third reference comes in a list of battles fought all over the 'old North' by one Gwallawg (XI.21).

> ... A battle near Bre Tryn, much heated,
> His fury a might fire;
> A battle before splendid ramparts,
> A hundred warbands trembled in Aeron ...
>   (Clancy 1998, 91)

In the context of the other sites mentioned in the poem, it is reasonable to identify the battle site of Bre Trwyn, 'the brae/upland of Troon' with the Dundonald Hills (Watson 1926, 342; Williams 1968, 123–4; Clancy 1998, 349) and perhaps Dundonald itself with the 'splendid ramparts'.

Aeron was the home of Cynon, whom John Koch has described as 'the single most important hero' in the *Gododdin* (1997, xli). The *Gododdin* focuses on battle deeds and the heroic qualities of the fallen warriors, most especially the bonds of loyalty, which were cemented through the celebrations in the mead hall. The great hall, of course, was the very place where these poems were subsequently performed, reinforcing the social values of loyalty and heroism. The celebration of Cynon's bloody deeds typifies the entire *Gododdin* corpus.

> A most fitting song for Cynon of the rightful privileges:
> He was slain; and before the defensive barrier of Aeron was laid waste,
> He reckoned [the deeds of] his gauntlet, measuring in grey eagles;
> [for] in urgency, he made food for scavengers.
> For the sake of the subject mounted warriors from the mountain country,
> He put his side in front of the spears(s) of enemies.
> Before Catraeth there were swift gold-torqued men;
> They slew; they cut down those would stand.
> The whelps of violence were [far] away from their [home] regions.
> A great rarity in battle on the side
> Of the Gododdin Britons was any [?]cavalryman superior to Cynon.
>   (Koch 1997, 23)

Elsewhere in the *Gododdin*, Cynon's praise is issued by his enemies, the Deirans of Northumbria, who were expanding into Ayrshire during the 7th and 8th centuries. 'Heathen tribes of Deiran brigands used to ask whether there came from the Britons a man better than Kynon' (Koch 1997, xxxix). By the mid 8th century, the Britons appear to have lost the struggle for Aeron, because the conquest of 'the plain of Kyle, with other districts by the Northumbrian king Eadberht is recorded in AD 750 in the Continuation of Bede's *Ecclesiastical History* (Anderson 1908, 56).

The modern district names of Kyle, Cunningham and Carrick (Fig 1), seem to have taken shape in the Early Historic period. Carrick's etymology is straightforward and less revealing; it derives from *carreg*, 'rock' (Watson 1926, 186), perhaps a reference to Ailsa Craig. According to W. J. Watson (1926, 186) the name Kyle commemorates the quasi-mythical 5th-century king *Coel Hen*, the apical figure of several northern (*Coeling*) dynasties, including that of Urien of Rheged. Cunningham is first mentioned in Bede's *Ecclesiastical History* (V.12)

'*Incuneningam*'. The -*ingham* ending indicates an Anglo-Saxon coining, but *t*
Cunen appears to be a British personal name and it is tempting to link him with
Cynon of Aeron who appears so prominently in the Gododdin poems. It should be
noted that Bede describes Cunningham as being *in provincia Nordanhynbrorum*
and *in regione Nordanhynbrorum*. While this could be a reference to the situation
at the time of writing (730s) it should be noted that the proangonist of the story,
which takes place in the 690s, has an Anglo-Saxon name, Drythelm. Either way
Bede's story indicates Anglo-Saxon settlement in Ayrshire.

The earliest attestation of the name Dundonald, 'fort of Donald', is found
in the 12th-century *Life of St Modwenna*, an English saint whose life had been
conflated with that of the Irish St Darerca (d. AD 517) (Bartlett 2002, xiv). The
place mentioned, *Dundeuenel,* has been widely accepted as Dundonald, although
Barrow for unstated reasons prefers a lost site in Galloway (2004, 5). In one
episode 'Modwenna' crosses the Irish Sea and visits a number of places in central
Scotland where she founds a chapel or more substantial church (Bartlett 2002, xvi,
122–3). The list includes Dumbarton, Stirling, Edinburgh and Traprain Law all
regional power centers of the northern Britons. That Dundonald (*Dundeuenel*)
is listed alongside these implies the author of the *Life* considered it as being of
similar importance. Bartlett argues that this strand of the *Life* was probably in
existence by the 11th century, as it is based on an Irish *Life* by Conchubranus but
recognises that it may draw upon an earlier *Life* composed in the 7th century
(Bartlett 2002, xiv–xv). Again Barrow is less inclined to recognise these early
strata and prefers to see the *Life* as a solely 12th-century composition. The
excavated evidence at Dundonald spans the 7th to 12th centuries and indicates that
it was probably sufficiently prominent throughout this time range to allow it to
have been included in a list of politically significant regional centres, whether it
was composed in the 7th or 12th century. The name itself, however, may hold a
clue to the local significance of the site.

The form of the name Dundonald found in the *Life of St Modwenna*,
'Dundeuenel', is consistent with it having been formed from British Dyfnwal
(*Din Dyfnwal), a name which is cognate with Gaelic Dòmhnall, anglicised as
Donald (T. O. Clancy, pers. comm.). This points to an association with the
Kynwydyon dynasty of Strathclyde who claimed decent from Dyfnwal Hen,
great-grandfather of Ryderch Hen (*flourit* AD 570–80). The name Dyfnwal was a *ð*
popular with this dynasty – one is attested in the 8th century and three between the
late 9th to late 10th centuries (cf. Broun 2004, 135) – although no link can be made
with a particular Dyfnwal it is tempting to see it as associated with one or other
member of this royal dynasty.

Tellingly, the region around Dundonald is deserving of a mention in a range
of sources over a long timespan, which suggests its regional importance is rooted
in the late Roman and Early Historic period. A great stability is indicated by the
name Kyle, which is one of the earliest British territorial units and the only one
(apart from Lothian) whose name is still in use in modern Scotland. The early
British poetry, such as the *Gododdin* elegies, captures something of the social
world of the warrior aristocracy at the heart of Early Historic political life. It is
entirely appropriate to the society celebrated in the *Gododdin* with the court at
Dumbarton, because of the indications that the collection was preserved for a time

in Strathclyde. Moreover it seems not unreasonable to speculate that some of the *Gododdin* poems were heard within the hall of Dundonald.

Political Context

When it comes to reconstructing the real political world inhabited by the occupants of Dundonald we are on shakier ground, because the prosaic legacy of the Britons is more meagre than the poetry. There are few contemporary British sources and most of what is known about political developments must be extracted from English and Gaelic materials (Anderson 1908; 1922; Kirby 1962). The uncertainties and gaps in the contemporary record impose severe limitations on the historian and militate against the construction of a coherent narrative. Nevertheless, since the Middle Ages, historians have sought to account for the decline and eventual disappearance of the northern British kingdoms and when the evidence has grown scarce, have fallen back on traditions first articulated by John of Fordun in the 14th century (Broun 2004, 130–35). The narrative tradition instigated by Fordun links the sack of Dumbarton by the Dublin Vikings in AD 870 with the final collapse of British political sovereignty. The political vacuum was then filled by the Gaelic kingdom of Alba, which came to dominate the kingdom of Strathclyde by the 10th century. By this time Strathclyde was a dependent sub-kingdom ruled by the designated heir of the king of Scots, in a manner suspiciously similar to the relationship between the king of England and the prince of Wales.

While there is every reason to accept that AD 870 indeed marks a major historical watershed, there can be less certainty that the Gaelic kingdom of Alba dominated the Clyde valley during the Viking Age. However, recent scholarship has refined our understanding of the extent of the pre-Viking kingdom of Dumbarton and of the nature of the Viking Age kingdom of Strathclyde. The arguments for a revision have been drawn together by Dauvit Broun (2004), who provides a historical analysis based upon penetrating source criticism. The arguments, while too involved to consider here, challenge the view of a rapid, terminal decline for the Britons and suggest that a British kingdom lasted in Strathclyde until late in the 12th century. As part of this revision Broun also seeks to separate the replacement of British speech by Gaelic from the development of the kingdom of Alba, in favour of linking the spread of Gaelic in Strathclyde to the influence of the *Gall Gaillib*.

A key point to emerge from this recent scholarly work is that the kingdom of Strathclyde, properly speaking, is a product of the post 870 political landscape (Clancy forthcoming). Prior to this date the kingdom was identified by both Britons and Gaels as 'Clyde Rock': Welsh *Al Clud* and Gaelic *Aíl Cluaithe*, referring to what is now Dumbarton, 'fort of the Britons'. This distinction between the kingdom of Dumbarton and that of Strathclyde is not simply a terminological nicety, but probably reflects a major political disruption, which was accompanied by a physical shift in the centre of power and a reconfiguration of the ruling elite. The best candidate for the new royal centre on the Clyde is found upstream from Dumbarton at Partick, which was on the opposite bank from the ancient church of Govan, probably the royal burial place (Driscoll 2003, 2004).

Over the years uncritical usage of the term Strathclyde and casual cartography have suggested that a single kingdom dominated all of west central Scotland, embracing modern Dunbartonshire, Lanarkshire, Renfrewshire and Ayrshire. That this vast area was a single polity now seems implausible. The contemporary references suggest, rather, that the pre-Viking kingdom of Clyde Rock encompassed an area embracing the Clyde similar to the later counties of Dunbartonshire and Renfrewshire (Clancy forthcoming). Apart from the three Ayrshire districts mentioned above (Kyle, Cunningham and Carrick), there is little indication of the political arrangements south of the Clyde, but the use of these names might suggest smaller-scale polities.

While the kingdom of Dumbarton survived until the 9th century, it may be that south of the Clyde the expanding Northumbrian kingdom had a corrosive effect on the local British polities. Aeron may have ceased to exist in the wake of Eadberht's conquest of Kyle in AD 752: But whether or not the British kingdoms survived, there was certainly a significant English settlement as indicated by the Anglo-Saxon place-names and ecclesiastical dedications found across the south-west. By the 8th century English was being spoken practically within earshot of the Clyde, to judge from the place-name Eaglesham. English ambition extended across the Clyde further as can be seen from the Pyrrhic victory at Dumbarton by combined Northumbrian and Pictish armies in AD 756 (Forsyth 2000). The long-term consequences of the Northumbrian presence for the Ayr region are difficult to assess, but the first mention of Dundonald in the company of Edinburgh, Stirling and so on, suggests that it was a regional power centre and as such would have been on the front line in the struggles first with the Northumbrians and later with the Vikings and the *Gall Gaillib*. On the face of it Dundonald appears to have been more successful in resisting the Viking onslaught of the 9th century than Dumbarton. But the collapse of the fort at *Al Clut* was not the end of the British kingdom on the Clyde. The British kingdom of Strathclyde which emerges after 870 may have even expanded, if its influence can be measured by the 10th- and 11th-century sculpture spread up and down the Clyde (Macquarrie 1990; Craig 1994; Driscoll *et al* in press). If the sculpture reflects political hegemony, then Dundonald appears to fall within its sphere of influence, given the presence of high-quality sculpture of this period at nearby Kilwinning (Craig 1994, 77–9)

A key point to emerge from Broun's analysis is that Strathclyde, despite the clear Viking influence in the earlier elements of the sculpture, continued to be ruled by Britons (Broun 2004, 125–30). Indeed there is no compelling case for regarding Strathclyde as a dependency or puppet of the Gaelic kingdom of Alba at this time. Instead of thinking of the main Gaelic influence coming from the east under the domination of Alba, Broun looks westward to the busy Irish Sea of the Viking Age. In his view the *Gall Gaellib* were more active on the Clyde coast than is generally appreciated, which is a relevant point given the proximity of Hunterston, findspot of the remarkable brooch with a Gaelic name scratched in runes on the back (Alcock 2003, 312–2). Although it is not possible to discern their political influence in detail the *Gall Gaellib* did leave their mark in the stratum of Gaelic place-names in Ayrshire and Renfrewshire.

By the 12th century the extent of Strathclyde was approaching the large area normally represented on maps produced by modern scholars (e.g. Hall and

Haywood 2001, 69). This great expansion, although widely recognised, is hard to reconcile with a British kingdom beset by Gaels on the east and west. One possibility is that Northumbria enjoyed another period of expansion north and west from the Borders during the 11th century and was somehow allied with Strathclyde (Broun 2004, 136–40). The brutal suppression of Northumbrians in 1070 by William I ended their northern aspirations and these extensive lands fell into the lap of the kings of Strathclyde, so that the last British kings enjoyed dominion over vast territories extending to the Solway and the Tweed.

Archaeological Neighbours

In many respects Dumbarton offers the closest archaeological parallel for Dundonald. Although Dumbarton has a richer documentary history, as befits a great regional centre, much more is known about the archaeology of Dundonald, because the Alcocks' excavations at Dumbarton were on a smaller scale (Alcock and Alcock 1990). Even so Dumbarton has produced an extremely informative assemblage of finds which points to its role as the major centre for long-distance trade in the region starting with 5th-century Mediterranean routes (exemplified by B-ware) and shifting in the 6th and 7th centuries to the Continent (E-ware). Trade within the Irish Sea of the Viking Age was presumably brisk before Dumbarton was destroyed in AD 870. After that the focal point for the Clyde seems to have shifted upstream to Partick-Govan, which at this time appears to have consisted of a group of inter-related sites straddling the river including the ancient church and an assembly place (Doomster Hill) at Govan on the south bank and a royal manor at Partick on the north (Driscoll 2003, 2004).

Closer to Dundonald, in Ayrshire there are three sites which have produced artefacts from the Early Historic period: the crannogs at Buiston and Lochlee (Munro 1882), and Castle Hill, Dalry (Alcock 2003, 325, 448). Buiston is certainly the most valuable of these for comparison, because of the wealth of artefacts discovered by Munro and because of the re-excavation of the site by Ann Crone (2000). The range of artefacts including Continetal and Anglo-Saxon imports, evidence for metalworking and organic materials, provides some indication of the materials that have not survived at Dundonald, while the timber-work reveals the architectural possibilities of the buildings otherwise known only from postholes.

With respect to the development sequence at Dundonald, perhaps the closest comparison is provided by Auldhill, Portencross. Here David Caldwell and his team excavated a hill which was fortified in prehistoric times and refurbished repeatedly using earth-and-timber works until these were replaced by the great masonry castle (Caldwell et al. 1998). Although Portencross is not on a comparable scale to Dundonald, conceptually and in practice the redevelopment sequence shows strong parallels with it.

Ecclesiastical Setting

There are suggestions of political coherence in the evidence for ecclesiastic organisation in this region. There seems little doubt that Christianity was taking root here by the 5th century as it was elsewhere in Britain (Clancy 2001, 10–11; see Taylor 1998 for a review the critical place-name evidence). The historical and linguistic evidence is reinforced by the recent discoveries of early Christian cemeteries on the Clyde at Govan (Driscoll 2004, 8) and Ardrossan (DES 2003, 96–7). Of particular relevance to understanding the organisation of the church in Strathclyde are the church dedications to the British St Uinniau (Finnian) who was active in the mid 6th century and was popular in the south-west: he is com- memorated at Kilwining, Beith, Dalry, Lochwinnoch and Inchinnan (Clancy 2001, 18). Collectively this group of dedications suggests a political dimension that may represent the cult of a saint favoured by a particularly successful dynasty. The parish church in Dundonald is dedicated to St Ninian, who was enjoying a period of popularity in the 12th-century, when the village is likely to have been established. However, as Clancy has revealed, a great deal of confusion has arisen over the centuries between Uinniau/Finnian and Ninian (Clancy 2001), so it is possible that an earlier church was dedicated to Uinniau.

There is a large volume of sculpture dating to the 9th and 10th century in northern Britain, with celebrated collections in Govan and Whithorn. While it is agreed that the corpus reflects the cultural mix of the Viking Age, just how this should be read is a matter of debate. It is interesting to note that three of the sites associated with Uinniau/Finnian – Kilwining, Lochwinnoch and Inchinnan – have sculpture from this period (Craig 1994, 77–8, 81, 89–90). If nothing else this sculpture suggests that the church managed to ride the political storms of the Viking Age. Indeed the relative absence of an interest in the lands in Ayrshire by the Bishop of Glasgow suggests that the influence of the ancient churches of Paisley and Kilwinning survived into the 12th century.

An Early Historic Royal Centre?

On a wide range of criteria, Dundonald meets our expectations of what an Early Historic royal site would be like (see Alcock 2003, 179–200). The form of the fortifications are readily paralleled elsewhere in Scotland. The presence of imported pottery and dye-stuffs, evidence for fine metal working and weapons are also to be expected on a royal site at this time (Campbell 1996). The scant historical record makes it impossible to comment on the sorts of events taking place there, but its history of destruction and reuse surely points to a place of lasting strategic and probably political significance. There seems little reason to doubt that Dundonald was the *caput* of Kyle, and we are probably justified in thinking of it as a royal centre, but how far its influence stretched in the Early Historic period is probably beyond speculation.

THE COMING OF THE STEWARTS

During the earliest period of the Anglo-Norman settlement, the lands of Dundonald, situated in the northern half of Kyle, formed part of the extensive estates of Walter, son of Alan. A charter of Malcolm IV issued in 1161 or 1162 refers to Walter as the king's steward (*dapifer* or *senescallus*) and makes it clear that the office (*senescalcia*) had been bestowed on him by Malcolm's grandfather,

David I. As steward, Walter the Stewart would have been in charge of the day-to-day running of the royal household and was in constant attendance at court, as may be seen from his witnessing of royal charters (cf. RRS I, 31–2). In addition to confirming to him David's grants of Renfrew, Paisley, Pollock, 'Talahret', Cathcart, Dripps, Mearns, Eaglesham, Lochwinnoch and Innerwick (East Lothian), Malcolm also granted Walter the demesne of Partick as well as Inchinnan, Stenton, Hassenden, Legerwood and Birkenside, and for his lodging a toft in every burgh and demesne in the land (RRS I, 225–6, no. 184).

It is not known for certain when or from whom Walter received the northern half of Kyle, which later came to be known as 'Kyle Stewart', or 'Walter's Kyle', as the royal charter that would have conferred it to him has not survived. Although no mention of this estate is made in Malcolm's charter of 1161–2, the witnesses to it include Gilbert, son of Richer, Walter's tenant in Tarbolton in Kyle. Walter's Kyle estate may therefore already have been in his hands by that date, having been granted him by David I or Malcolm IV (cf. RRS I, 286, no. 310; cf. 39). A date around this time also appears likely for other reasons. A feature of the reigns of David I and Malcolm IV was the creation of large fiefs in the south-west of the kingdom to strengthen the western approaches against attack from Galloway, the Isle of Man and the Western Isles and gradually bring them under royal control. Cunningham, for example, with its *caput* at Irvine, was probably created by David I between 1136 and 1153, and was certainly in the hands of Hugh de Morville by *c.* 1162 (Barrow 1980, 46, 58–9, 62, 72 n.64).

In 1159, Walter the Stewart had accompanied Malcolm IV on an expedition to France with Henry II of England. On his return, Malcolm faced a revolt led by Earl Ferteth, who with five other earls besieged the king in Perth. When the coup failed, the rebels took refuge in Galloway, where the king pursued them with three armed expeditions (Anderson 1922 I, 244–5). Although the names of those who accompanied Malcolm are not recorded, it seems reasonable to assume that Walter the Stewart would have been among them. Another threat to the stability of the realm was posed by the rise of Somerled, a Gallo-Norse leader, who carved out an extensive lordship for himself on the western seaboard at the expense of the Norse kingdom of Man and the Isles. In the 1150s he made a bid for power in alliance with the sons of Malcolm Macheth. Although the attempt failed, Somerled remained a threat to the Scottish kingdom until he was finally defeated and killed at Renfrew in 1164. The Melrose chronicle relates:

> Somerled, the under-king (*regulus*) of Argyll, who had been in a state of wicked rebellion for twelve years against his natural lord, Malcolm, king of Scotland, landed at Renfrew, with a large army which he had collected together in Ireland and various places; but at length God's vengeance overtook him, and he and his son (Gillabrighte), and a countless number of his followers, were there slain by a few people of that district. (Stevenson 1988, 13; cf. Anderson 1922 II, 254–5)

It seems more than probable that the royal forces on this occasion were commanded by Walter the Stewart, who held the fee of Renfrew from the king.

Although Walter chose Renfrew around 1163 as the location for the priory that a few years later was to merge into the new abbey of Paisley (Cowan and Easson

1976: 64–5; Barrow 1980, 67), such religious patronage does not necessarily mean that he regarded Renfrew as his main *caput*. In a later grant of various lands and churches to the priory at Renfrew, the Stewart donated the tithe 'of all my rents from all my lands except Kyle'. In contrast to the lavish grants that he made elsewhere, those that he made within Kyle were relatively modest, amounting to no more than a piece of land in the later parish of Monkton and the church of Prestwick (Innes 1832, 6). This lends support to the view that it was in Kyle that he retained his largest unit of demesne land. In fact it was not until 1222–38 that Walter's grandson, Walter II, donated the churches of Dundonald (with its chapels of Crosby and Riccarton), Senechar and Auckinlek to Paisley Abbey (Innes 1832, 18). Since such donations would only have been made from the demesne land of the Stewart, this also suggests that Walter I and his successors retained a significant amount of demesne in Kyle, including Dundonald itself, and significantly more than in any of his other mainland fiefs.

Other evidence also suggests that Kyle, and Dundonald in particular, held special prominence among Walter's fiefs. In one of his charters, dated *c*. 1163–70, there is listed among the witnesses a man named 'Richard, my clerk' (*Ricardo clerico meo*) (Innes 1832, 6). The same clerk appears in various charters that were either made by or witnessed in the presence of Walter or his son, Alan; but in other charters associated with Walter and Alan that were made in their absence, Richard is described as 'clerk of Dundonald' (*clerico de Dundonald*, or *Dundouneaud*) (Innes 1832, 99 and 113). This suggests at the very least that an important member of the Stewarts' administrative staff was actually based at Dundonald, where he possibly also served as chaplain.

In view of its significance among the Stewarts' fiefs and the position that it occupied as as *caput* of Kyle Stewart, it is highly probable that Dundonald would have been provided with a castle of some sort, if not during the lifetime of Walter I then most certainly during the time when his son, Alan, was Stewart (1177–1204). It was during this period, in 1197, that a new royal castle was erected at Ayr (Barrow 1980, 46; Anderson 1922, II, 348). In 1234, during the period when Alan's successor, Walter II (1204–41), was acting as Stewart of Scotland (*senescallus*), the Gallovidians rose in revolt and, according to the Melrose Chronicle, 'devastated with fire and sword some of the royal lands contiguous to themselves' (Stevenson 1988, 60–1; Anderson 1980, II, 494–5). Kyle Regis may well have been the area affected by this incursion; and, when King Alexander II led an army into Galloway to crush the rising the following year (Anderson 1980, II, 495–8), Kyle Stewart and its lord may be expected to have played a significant strategic and logistical role. Among the witnesses to Walter II's charters we find Nicolas, the parson of Dundonald (*persona de Dundovenald*), and his brother William (Innes 1832, 19 and 40).

Alexander, the 4th Stewart of Scotland (1241–83), who defeated the Norwegians at Largs in 1263, was also sometimes referred to as Alexander 'of Dundonald' (RMS I, 509 n.2). However, no mention is made of any castle at Dundonald, before the late 13th century. One of the first references is made by an unreliable source, the 17th-century historian Hugh Macdonald, who relates how Angus, lord of the Isles, assisted Robert I in holding Dundonald against the English during the Wars of Independence (Macphaill 1914, I, 14–16). The first certain mention of the castle is in a charter dated between *c.* 1283 and 22 July 1298, by which James, 5th Stewart, granted some land near the castle to the clerk, William 'del Schaw' (Dillon 1966, 32–6; Barrow and Royan 1985, 182). The lack of any documentation before this period, however, is by no means unique in the study of Scottish castles. Many major castles known through excavation or by other means to have been in existence in the 13th century or earlier fail similarly to appear in any written record (Fig 4).

James Stewart forfeited his lands, including Dundonald, on 31 August 1298, following his support of William Wallace during the Wars of Independence. They were granted by King Edward I to Sir Alexander Lindsay and others, and then within the same year to Henry de Lacy, earl of Lincoln (CDS II, 257, no. 1006; cf. Barrow 1976, 144 n.1; Barrow and Royan 1985, 177–8). Although James Stewart submitted himself to the king's will and regained his estates in November 1305 (CDS II, 463, no. 1713), they were soon back again in the hands of de Lacy, who held them until 23 October 1306, when James Stewart again submitted himself to Edward I at Lanercost Priory in Westmorland (CDS II, 494, no. 1843; 496, no 1857; cf. Barrow 1976, 189, 217–8; Barrow and Royan 1985, 180).

James's brother, William le fiz le Stywarde, had paid homage to Edward I at Berwick on 28 August 1296 (CDS II, 203). He evidently continued to serve the king during the latter's Scottish war, but was fined a 'rauncun' of £50 for harbouring his brother against the king's peace. In the petition that he sent to Edward in 1307, asking for a partial remission of his unpaid fine in consideration of his good service, he is named William Dundonald (CDS IV, 381, no. 1836). William had most likely inherited this name from his father, Alexander of Dundonald, though it is more difficult to say whether this should be taken to mean that he actually held the castle of Dundonald at any time.

The Royal Castle

The lordship of Dundonald often seems to have been held by one of the Stewart's sons, usually, though not always, the eldest. During the 1360s, for example, while Robert the Stewart (later King Robert II) was holding the earldom of Strathearn, his eldest son and heir, John Stewart (later Robert III), was known as lord of the barony of Kyle (*dominus barronie de Kyle*) (Innes 1832, 29 and 69; cf. RMS, I 177–8, no. 491 [1369]). Dundonald continued to play an important role after Robert II's accession to the throne in 1371. We find him issuing charters there in early December of that year (RMS I, 135–6, no. 378; 138, no. 392; 145, no. 407; 154–6, no. 428; 197, no. 540) and again on 25 December 1389 (RMS, 303, no. 803). According to the early 15th-century chronicler Andrew of Wytoun, Robert II's death on 19 April 1390 occurred 'at Dundownald in his cuntre' (Laing 1879, 44; Amours 1908, 264–5), while Walter Bower, writing of the same event in the 1440s, specifically mentions that the king died in the castle (Watt 1993, VII, 446; cf. Nicholson 1974, 203–4).

Robert II's successor, Robert III, also made frequent visits to Dundonald (Fig 5). He issued charters there in March 1391 (RMS I, 303, nos 803–4), July 1391 (RMS I no. 836), February 1393 (RMS II 516, no. 2429), November 1404 (RMS II 87, no. 378), January 1405 (RMS II no. 379; 92–3, no. 403), and October 1405.

Fig 4 The site from the SE with conservation scaffolding in position.

Fig 5 The site from the NE at the time of the excavations.

Wyntoun claims that Robert III also died at Dundonald, on 4 April 1406 (Amours 1908, vi, 415), but other sources, including Bower, record on better authority that he died in his castle of Rothesay, on the Isle of Bute (Watt, VIII, 62, 177 and 178; ER III, xcv–xcvi). John Stewart, the natural brother both of the late king and of the guardian of the realm, Robert, duke of Albany, is referred to in 1407 and 1415 as John Stewart of Dundonald. This designation may simply mean that he had been born there; but it could equally well indicate that he was holding the castle after his father's death (RMS I, 380, no. 900; RMS 650, app. 2, no. 1976).

James I seems to have taken the castle into his own hands when he returned from exile in England in 1424. In 1426, on the king's authority, £16.13s.4d. was paid from the account of the custumars and bailiffs of Ayr to Fergus Kennedy for repairing the king's castle at Dundonald and the park there (ER IV, 401). The account rendered for the period May 1433–June 1434 by Thomas Kennedy, bailiff of the royal estates in Carrick and elsewhere, including Dundonald, gives the annual income from the lands of Dundonald as £47.17s.8d., a value that was to remain relatively stable over the next fifty years. Out of this sum the following payments were recorded in the same account: 13d.4d. (one merk) from the lands of the *Holme* given in alms, as from ancient times, to the chaplain who celebrated in the chapel of St Ninian, near the castle (*prope castrum*); £1.6s.8d. for the royal park of Dundonald; £3 to the gatekeeper and two watchmen in the castle; £2 for mowing the meadow of Dundonald and making hay; and £1.1s.9d. for the wages of the stable-hands who cared for the king's horses during the period of the account (ER III, 594–6).

The comptroller's account for 1449–50 records the receipt of a grassum payment of £12 from Gilbert Kennedy for his entry into the lands of Dundonald (ER V, 395). As bailiff for the earldom of Carrick, Kennedy rendered a series of accounts for the royal lands of Dundonald from July 1450 until July 1479 (ER V–X, *passim*). For most of that period the annual income due from Dundonald was £49.0s.8d. Out of this, £16.6s.8d. was paid annually to Alan, Lord Cathcart, for lands in Dundonald that he held in feu from the king. The residue of £32.14s. seems from the start to have been withheld by Kennedy himself and was only mentioned in the accounts presented from 1456–7 onwards, although in that year the sum was accidentally given (at least in the published version) as £31.14s. Of this withheld sum, eleven merks (£7.6s.8d.) were to be paid to the chaplain, while the remainder, which in normal years would have been £25.7s.4d., was retained by the comptar (ER VI, 341–3; ER VII, 27, 388, 450, 562). In the account for 1468–69, the short paragraph that had been inserted since 1456–7 to explain this withheld money was expanded to include the additional detail that the sum retained by the comptar himself was in respect of his custody of the castle (*pro custodia castri*) (ER VII, 646); and, in the 1473–4 account, the chaplain is described as 'celebrating in the chapel of Dundonald' (ER VIII, 297). It is probable that Gilbert Kennedy had been keeper of the castle from the time of his first entry into the Dundonald lands, despite the apparent lack of any other record to that effect. In the account for 1467–8, however, he is referred to as Lord Kennedy, bailiff of Carrick (ER VII, 562–4), and in the following one for 1468–9 he is styled Lord Kennedy, king's chamberlain in the county of Carrick and lord of Dundonald (ER VI, 646–7). In addition to the normal payments made to Lord Cathcart, to the chaplain and to Lord Kennedy himself, the account for 1466–7 also included a sum of £3 paid from other sources to the comptar for the expense of imprisoning certain wrongdoers in the castle of Dundonald, on the king's orders (ER, VII, 452).

LATE MEDIEVAL TENANTS AND TACKSMEN

From 1477, Gilbert Kennedy's accounting in respect of Dundonald began to fall into arrears, apparently because of the non-payment or non-collection of rents (ER, VIII, 404–6, 512–13, 614–15). When his son, John, succeeded him as Lord Kennedy and chamberlain of Carrick in 1481, he inherited more than £100 of arrears, even after £64.15s.4d. had been effectively written off (ER VIII, 614–15; IX, 122–3). The arrears continued to mount in succeeding years (ER IX, 195–6, 273–4, 408–9, 495–7), until in the account for 1487–8 there is no mention of Dundonald at all (ER X, 16–18). The reason why John, Lord Kennedy, was unable to put the Dundonald accounts in order after his father's death seems to have been that the castle and lands were either never under his control or, if they were, quickly passed out of it. For in December 1482, James III had granted the custody of the castle to Alan, Lord Cathcart, on the same terms on which it had earlier been held by John Ross of Montgrenane, namely for the tenure in free barony and in feu for 1s. a year of the domain lands of Dundonald (Dundownald) and the lands of Balrassy, Parkthorn, Auchinche, Bogside, Galriggs and Gudelandis in Kyle Stewart (RMS II, 320, no. 1530).

In the account for August 1488–August 1489, John Kennedy was finally excused answering for the lands of Dundonald, 'because John Wallace of Craigie has custody of its castle and is occupying the lands of its barony, for which he is answerable' (ER X, 125). The arrears from the years 1477–82, amounting to £227.11s.4d., were eventually written off in 1492 (ER X, 327–8).

In the years following, the lands of Dundonald were let to a succession of tacksmen. From 20 July 1508 they were let for eight years to the Lord Lyon King of Arms; but on his death, they were let on similar terms, on 6 December 1512, to Sir David Hume of Wedderburn and his son, George. As well as the lands mentioned in 1482, they included the Mains and the Reedbog mill and meadow (ER XIII, 656–7). Hume was forfeited in 1518, and on 16 June the lands were thereupon leased for five years to Mr John Campbell of Thorntoun, treasurer, and his wife Isabella (ER XIV, 347, 487). Campbell had relinquished the lease by 30 January 1520, when William Wallace, the tutor (or guardian) of Craigie, and his wife, Elizabeth Campbell, took seisin for the rest of the term (ER XIV, 455, 487). On 15 August 1526, Wallace was granted the feu of the lands of Dundonald, including the mill, woods and castle (*cum molendino, silvis et fortalicio*), thereby increasing his security of tenure (RMS III, 82, no. 367). Following Wallace's death, the estate passed in May 1531 to his son, William (ER XVI, 490, 534). On 20 May 1536, however, after the death of William Wallace junior, James V granted the lands and castle of Dundonald to Robert Boyd of Kilmarnock and his wife Helen Somerville, revoking the earlier grant made during his minority to William Wallace senior (RMS III, 353, no. 1583; 371, no. 1668). Boyd, however, was unable to evict the sitting tenants, despite making two attempt to do so by force in 1538 and 1541. In 1543, he therefore resigned his rights in favour of John Wallace, tutor of Craigie (ER XVIII, 35), though it was not until 1545 that Wallace and his wife, Katherine Kennedy, received charters of confirmation (RMS III, 737, no. 3136; 740, no. 3151). In April 1543, John Wallace also obtained a grant of the glebe, manse and other ploughlands associated with the chapel of St Ninian in Dundonald from the chaplain, Thomas Hucheson (RMS VII, 569, no. 1578).

John Wallace is recorded paying £40 in feuferm for Dundonald in 1558 (ER XIX, 76); but from 1564 until 1573 the lands were in the hands of the crown (ER XIX, 429). Another John Wallace of Dundonald took seisin in January 1573 (ER XIX, 429), and in October of that year and again in March 1575 he and his wife, Agnes Stewart, received feu charters for the domain lands in Dundonald known as Burnside (RMS IV, 564, no. 2149; 640, no. 2381). The castle and the lands associated with the chaplainry remained in the hands of the Wallace family until the early 17th century (RMS VIII, 652–3, no. 1916 [1632]). By 1588–9, however, John Wallace of Dundonald had moved residence to nearby Auchans Castle, which had been in the family's possession since 1527 (ER XXII, 25, 112, 187).

THE DEMISE OF THE CASTLE

From the 1590s onwards, all estate business was conducted at Auchans. Dundonald, however, continued to be used as an occasional lockup for local minor offenders. In 1607, for example, a woman was confined for two days and two nights in the castle for 'a relapse in the usual offence' (Gillespie 1939, 335). The evidence of wills and charters also indicates that Auchans remained the Wallace family's principal residence from this period (NAS GD8/379; NAS RS11/3, fols 255r–255v; NAS CC8/8/27, fols 214v–216r).

In 1632, burdened by debt, John Wallace's grandson, Matthew Wallace, was obliged to sell the lands of Dundonald to James Mathieson. In 1638, however, the lands of Dundonald, including the manse, glebe, arable land and meadow associated with the chaplainry of St Ninian, were sold to Sir William Cochrane of Cowdon. Charles I's charter of 5 March, which confirmed Cochrane and his wife, Euphenia Scott, as joint feu-holders, also erected the kirktoun of Dundonald into a free burgh and granted Cochrane the right to elect the bailiffs and to build a tolbooth and market cross (RMS VIII, 289–90, no. 805). Cochrane also acquired Auchans Castle, which he appears to have extended in 1644 (MacGibbon and Ross 1887, II, 179). It was there, in May 1648, that he settled the lands of Dundonald on his wife, during her lifetime (RMS IX, 735, no. 1979). Cochrane was granted the title Lord Cochrane of Dundonald in 1647 (RMS IX, 702, no. 1885) and became the first earl of Dundonald in 1669; he died and was buried at Dundonald in 1686. The estate was sold by the sixth earl in 1726, but he retained the castle, which by then was quite ruinous.

On 1 November 1773, the castle was visited by Dr Samuel Johnson, accompanied by James Boswell, who has left us the following account of their visit:

As we passed very near the castle of Dundonald, which was one of the many residences of the kings of Scotland, and in which Robert the Second lived and died, Dr Johnson wished to survey it particularly. It stands on a beautiful rising ground, which is seen at a great distance on several quarters, and from whence there is an extensive prospect of the rich district of Cunninghame, the western sea, the isle of Arran, and a part of the northern coast of Ireland. It has long been unroofed; and, though of considerable size, we could not, by any power of imagination, figure it as having been a suitable habitation for majesty. Dr Johnson, to irritate my old Scottish enthusiasm, was very jocular on the homely accommodation of 'King Bob', and roared and laughed till the ruins echoed. (Boswell 1796, 392)

The castle was scheduled in 1920. After some concern about decay of the fabric and misuse for agricultural purposes, it was finally placed in State guardianship by the earl of Dundonald in 1953. A campaign of restoration then commenced, a notable feature of the work being the narrow-gauge railway which ascended the hill to transport materials to the site. The *Evening Times* for 1 March 1955 reported on the work:

Home of royalty at one time, 800-year-old Dundonald Castle is showing alarming signs of its great age. Deep cracks are slitting the thick walls, and the whinstone which forms its massive structure is crumbling as the lime, which binds it, rots. To preserve it for the nation, the Ancient Monuments Division of the Ministry of Works has taken over.

Men skilled in the delicate work of preserving buildings of great age have moved in, hauling their whin dust, cement and tools up the 800ft hill to the castle by means of a small-gauge rail track.

It was in conjunction with this work that a programme of archaeological excavation was undertaken in 1986–8 and 1993. The Friends of Dundonald took over visitor management, opening a visitor centre in 1997, while Historic Scotland retains responsibility for conservation of the fabric.

3   The Excavations

After a short exploratory excavation in 1986, two seasons of extensive excavation were completed in 1987 and 1988. This work ran alongside the programme of repair and consolidation of the standing remains undertaken by Historic Scotland.

EXCAVATION STRATEGY

The early seasons of excavation concentrated on the area within the visible remains of the barmkin wall and an area immediately to the east (Trenches A, B, C, H and J; Fig 6). These large trenches were augmented by a series of narrower cuttings sited on either side of the approach route to the castle (Trenches D, E, F, G and I; Fig 6).

Fieldwork was resumed for a single short season in 1993 when Trench K was opened.

Trench A

This was the continuation of a narrow trial excavation completed in 1986, in order to establish the maximum depth of rubble within the inner courtyard, to the south-east of the tower and east of the south annexe. Excavation during 1987 cleared the area around the base of the S annexe, the interior of the eastern ground-floor chamber and the assumed pit prison.

Trench B

This covered a large area of the southern sector of the outer courtyard. Excavation here revealed evidence of a sequence of timber buildings: large round houses followed by a series of hall-like structures, all succeeded by several stone courtyard buildings.

Trench C

A long narrow trench was dug immediately beyond the E section of the barmkin wall, principally to expose the outer face of the wall for later consolidation. Excavation exposed the remains of a vitrified timber-laced rampart, lying very close to the line of the later medieval barmkin wall.

Trenches D and E

These trenches were excavated in 1987 and were intended to assess the remains of a possible defended route into the castle on the S side of the present pathway. The trenches exposed the southern tower of a twin-towered gatehouse.

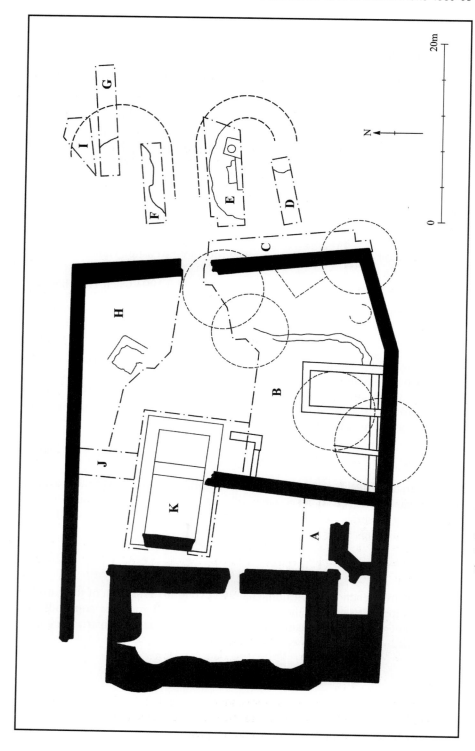

Fig 6 Plan of extant castle structures and location of excavations (trenches A–K).

Trenches F, G and I

These trenches were excavated in 1988 in order to complete the investigation of the heavily robbed-out gatehouse. Evidence was found of the northern tower, overlying the remains of a large earthwork, possibly a motte.

Trenches H and J

These cuttings covered the N side of the outer courtyard and brought to light fragmentary remains of a timber palisade and a large open cistern.

Trench K

Excavation continued in the area of a series of standing walls close to the northeast corner of the main tower and the N end of the E wall of the inner courtyard. This exercise revealed a series of stone buildings both predating and postdating the construction of the inner courtyard wall.

All the excavations were constrained by the existence of a light railway, running up the E side of the hill and operated by a winch in the castle courtyard, by which equipment and materials were supplied to the masons undertaking the conservation work. A further inhibiting factor in the successful excavation of such large areas in a relatively short time within the barmkin wall, was spoil disposal. Due to the difficulties in removing debris from the top of the hill, spoil was relocated several times by hand around the site over the two main seasons of work, until a suitable means of final removal was devised after excavation was completed.

SUMMARY OF MAIN PHASES OF OCCUPATION

Period 1   c. 1500–c. 500 BC
  Prehistoric kilns/ovens, indicating prehistoric activity on the site.

Period 2   c. 500 BC–c. AD 1000
  Iron Age to Early Historic hillfort with round timber buildings, gradually developing into dun-like complex with straight-sided buildings enclosed by a drystone rampart, later vitrified. In the 9th century, possibly the residence of a king of Strathclyde.

Period 3   c. 1000–1241
  Anglo-Norman colonisation: motte and bailey castle established. Timber hall and possible tower built by Walter Fitzalan, 1st Stewart.

Period 4   1241–c. 1300
  Castle of enclosure built by Alexander of Dundonald, 3rd Stewart. The complex comprised two opposing twin-towered gatehouses with linking rampart, describing a roughly trapezoidal plan.

Period 5   *c.* 1300–1371
  Destruction, repair and destruction during and after the Wars of Independence.
  The proposed sequence is:
  1. Destroyed by Robert Bruce, 1298.
  2. Refurbished by the Henry de Lacy, earl of Lincoln, for Edward I,
     1298–1301.
  3. Destroyed again by John de Soules, guardian of the kingdom, 1301.
  4. Abandoned, possibly until later 14th century.

Period 6   1371–1449/50
  Tower-house and barmkin built by Robert II, with barmkin buildings added
  later. Probably held by a keeper, with royal visits recorded until the 1430s.

Period 7   1449/50–1588/9
  Keepership held by Gilbert Kennedy, bailiff of Carrick, until 1481, and then
  by others until 1488/9, when it and the barony passed to John Wallace of
  Craigie. Except for the years *c.* 1500-20, when the lands were let to tacksmen,
  and 1536-43, when the feu was held by Robert Boyd of Kilmarnock, the
  Wallaces held Dundonald in feu until 1588/9.

Period 8   1588/9–1638
  The Wallaces move to Auchans Castle near by. Gradual decline of fabric and
  importance of castle.

Period 9   1638–1953
  Site abandoned when bought by Sir William Cochrane, later earl of
  Dundonald. Stone robbed from castle to enlarge Auchans Castle.

Period 10   1953–present
  Monument in State care.

PERIOD 1: SETTLEMENT, *c.* 1500–*c.* 500 BC (Fig 7)

A series of shallow soil deposits forming a slight mound extending 3m E–W by
3.8m N–S was revealed directly overlying the bedrock towards the extreme NE
corner of Trench B. This series [841] was characterised by high charcoal content
and some scattered bone, but most noticeably by scattered fragments of crude
pottery. In all, over 200 sherds from similar vessels were retrieved from this
surface (see p. 88). Generally referred to as 'very coarse pottery', it was hand-
made (i.e. not wheel-thrown), unglazed, with thick walls (up to 25mm) and large,
coarse, gritty inclusions. Its extremely fragile nature and its general lack of
distinction posed problems of interpretation, not least of which was whether the
assemblage reflected several vessels or only one. Given the relatively discrete
spread of the pottery, the evidence suggests that it was a single large pot, the
deposition of which coincided with the spreading of fire debris [841]. The latter
was spread in successive horizons, which subsequently slumped, giving rise in
part to the mounded profile of the deposit. The lowest of these spreads [1005]

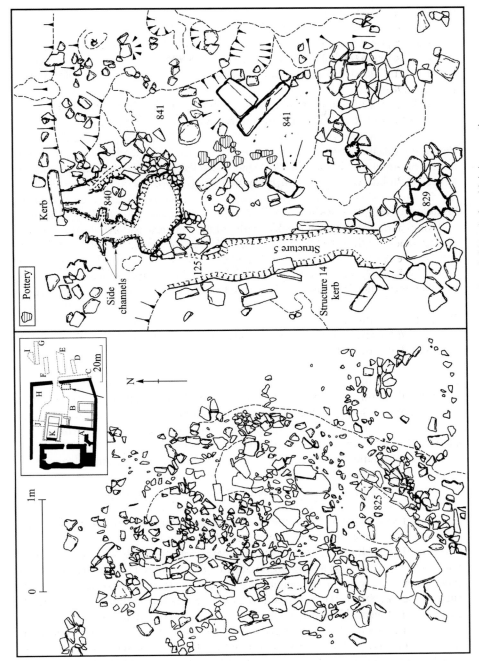

Fig 7 Plan of Period 1 [and 2?] features in Trench B before (left) and after (right) excavation.

yielded pottery which was subjected to thermoluminescence analysis at SURRC yielding an estimated firing date between 1500 and 500 BC (1030 ± 490 BC).

The most prominent structures associated with the pottery scatter and burnt deposits were two rounded shallow depressions [825, 840], enclosed by rings of small pitched stones with diameters of some 0.75m and 0.60m respectively. Despite having a similar fill of burnt clay and burnt stone, depression [825] proved to be far less well defined than [840], suggesting that it had served a different function. The pitched stones in both features may have been the remains of slightly domed roofs, but in view of its fragile nature it is equally possible that [825] merely represented the base of an eroded or robbed open hearth. It was clear that both structures had been destroyed and the resulting debris spread around the fringes of the slight eminence that they occupied.

It is likely that this, the earliest evidence for occupation, survived because it was destroyed and levelled shortly before the construction of overlying structures, and was buried directly beneath the levelling material for the floors of those buildings.

Feature [840]

This feature comprised an L-shaped channel, the contents of which showed the effects of heat, although no evidence of burnt materials associated with the source of this heat was revealed. The evidence suggested that there was some form of heat transfer from an external source, by blowing in some way up into the channel or flue. The fill of the channel contained residual elements of the superstructure and included burnt stone. Further, but slighter evidence of how the structure operated was suggested by a second, less substantial channel lying slightly to the E. Although shallow, it too had a distinctive L-shape, and together the two channels defined a triangular area. The suggestion that they were indeed part of the same structure was further implied by the presence of a large pitched stone lying across the openings of both, suggesting a kerb or a threshold (Fig 7).

Occupation debris from the complex sequence of buildings erected in Period 2 together with the narrow, banded nature of the associated contexts from Period 1 complicated the interpretation of this feature. This was compounded by the fact that much of the Period 2 debris in and around the later Period 4 E gatehouse was removed from the old hill summit and found its way into the backfill behind the E gatehouse towers (see below).

However, a small well-stratified assemblage was identified, potentially linked with the activities at and around feature [840]. This included two flints (SF 92 and 98), a crudely worked quartz fragment (SF 90), three shale spacer beads (SF 41, 110, 117) and a fragment of clay crucible (SF 126). This small group and the mass of coarse pottery and generally heat-affected debris suggests that feature [840] served either as a simple clamp kiln over a complex flue arrangement for smelting, or as an oven, possibly similar to the 'Tandoor' variety.

The main channel was found to be 1m long by 0.2m wide and featured two groups of two distinctive side channels, one 0.15m long, 0.8m wide, tapering to points; the other 0.8m long and 0.4m wide. These appear to have acted as a means of blocking the flue, rather like a gate or a sluice, presumably to control airflow once the chamber was hot enough.

The second flue did not feature side channels and ran for 0.80m, opening into an area of pitched small stones. Although the two flues were never linked, the similarity in plan and the shared access/entry point suggests at least that they represent phases of this same process. The main channel may also be regarded as a flue leading to the inner chamber or bowl, the latter being lozenge-shaped and measuring 0.95m by 0.45m.

Feature [825] – A Hearth?

Feature [825] lay 2.2m south of feature [840] and was defined on its SE side by a low bank of pitched stones, approximately 1m long by 0.4m wide. The eastern edge was truncated by a post-hole from Structure 6 (see below) and the pitched stones and pottery scatter defined a circular setting deformed to one side. The feature was interpreted tentatively as a hearth site.

PERIOD 2A: THE IRON AGE FORT, c. 500 BC–AD c. 600 (Figs 8–12)

All the main periods of occupation were represented only in very few places on the hill. This stratigraphic depth was most apparent on the highest point of the natural hill, which during Period 2 was extended by constructing a large artificial mound (Structure 17, pp. 35–8) to accommodate a series of round buildings.

The partial remains of six large round buildings were found in Trench B at the very heart of the early site (Figs 9 and 10). Although their chronological relationship is unknown, it is likely that no more than three stood at any one time. The structures are described in three groups (I–III), corresponding to the three areas or building terraces that they occupied. They represent only the most obvious of a potentially much more complex sequence of building on each platform, but even these six were by no means well preserved. All the main timber buildings from Period 2 were truncated by the line of the Period 6 barmkin wall, which represented the limits of the area available for excavation.

Group I, Structure 4

Structure 4 was the earliest timber structure and lay towards the middle of Trench B. It was defined by a ring of post-holes, 8.5m in diameter with an entrance facing south-east. It was interpreted as a roundhouse.

The interior of Structure 4 comprised levelled bedrock, which sustained patchy burning in an area towards the middle of the building, probably indicating the hearth setting. The entrance was marked by a roughly rectangular paved threshold [075] with two post settings [148 and 150] defining the doorway itself. The other main distinctive feature of this structure was a partition wall [233] running roughly NE to SW, dividing the interior in half. Finds included horse and cattle bones and a rubbing stone (SF 59).

Group I, Structure 1

This structure was 9m in diameter and was located towards the south-west of

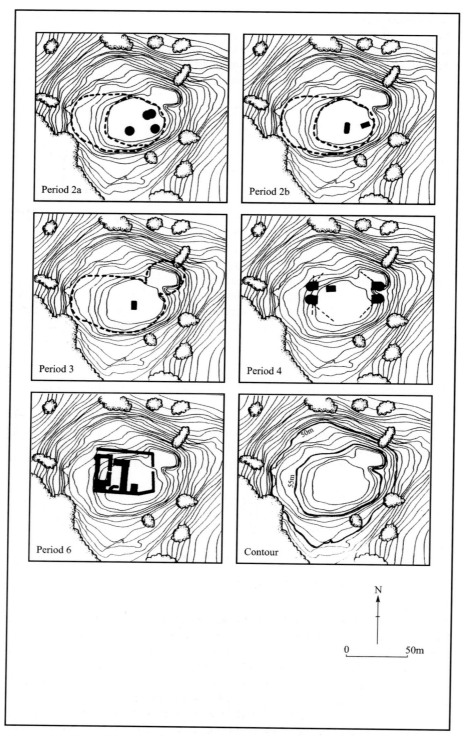

Fig 8 Developmental sequence for Periods 2–6. Dashed lines represent
conjectural defences.

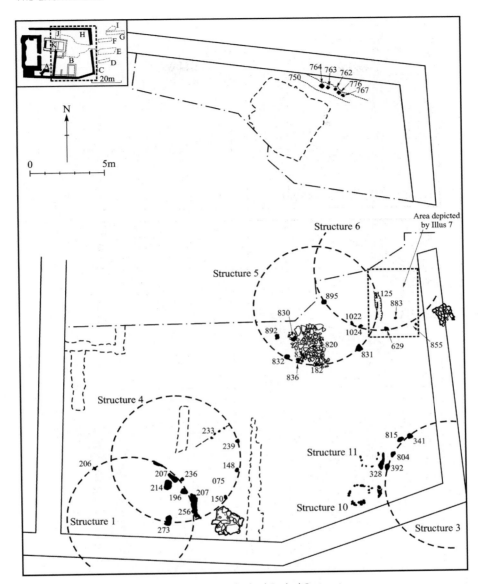

Fig 9 Plan showing principal Period 2 structures.

Trench B. Although most of the southern half of the building had been removed by the Period 6 barmkin wall, enough survived to identify a curved wall trench with intermittent uprights [207] defining the outer wall. The entrance faced NE and was represented by three posts [236, 214 and 196]. The whole structure was built over the levelled remains of Structure 4, which were partially sealed by an extensive metalled surface [180] on the SE side of the earlier building.

Numerous cattle bones were found in association with Structure 1, as well as many burnt bone fragments, all suggestive of cooking and food preparation debris.

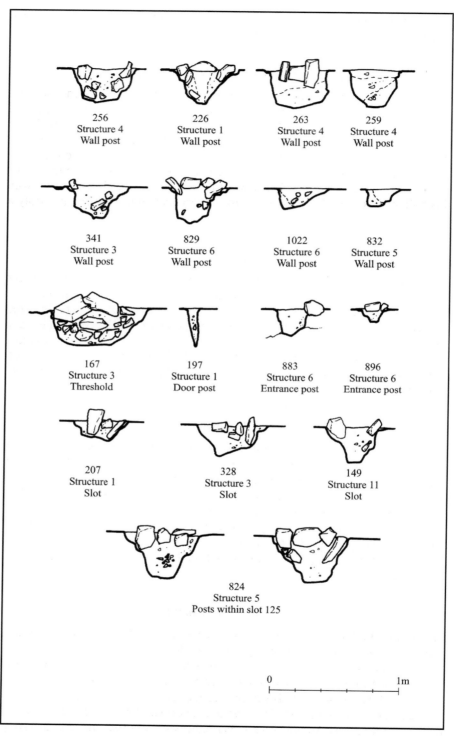

Fig 10 Sections of Period 2 post pits and settings.

Other finds included a bronze ring/brooch (SF 44) and a hook-like object, which may have been a strike-a-light (SF 45).

Group II, Structure 3

At the extreme south-eastern corner of Trench B, the north-western quadrant of a large round timber building was found. The building was of similar size and construction to Structure 1, featuring wall slots [328] flanking a W-facing entrance. The slots contained large posts, forming the main outer wall; an inner line of smaller posts was also revealed [392, 804, 815, 341]. Although badly damaged by the construction of the E barmkin wall in Period 6, enough of the building survived to suggest that it was 9m in diameter. Finds associated with this building included burnt bone, coarse pottery and an iron object, probably a nail.

Group II, Structure 10

A mass of small stake-holes and post-holes truncated the features and surfaces associated with Structure 3. These appeared to reflect two small rounded structures, which were of slight construction and may have been frequently repaired (Structures 10 and 11, Fig 9). Of the two, Structure 10 had a discrete ground plan, comprising two concentric rings of post or stake settings, defining a structure c. 2.25m in diameter. There was no obvious trace of floors or occupation surfaces, and this fact, coupled with the small size of the building, indicated that it was not a domestic building.

Group II, Structure 11

This configuration of small post-pits and stake-holes had a less obvious building plan than Structure 10 and the phasing was also less clear. However, the grouping was similar in character and in overall dimensions to Structure 10. The small size of the posts, as indicated by the post settings, suggests the use of very light timber, perhaps even some form of wicker or wattle construction. Such a building, especially if repaired periodically, would result in a mass of pits laid out in a roughly circular pattern, as was found here.

The finds retrieved in association with this rather nebulous structure consisted of cattle and dog bones.

Group III, Structure 6

The residual Period 1 occupation surface was overlain in Period 2 by the building platform for a round timber building (Structure 6, Figs 9 and 11).

Structure 6 was very similar to Structure 4, featuring a paved threshold [855] and a wall line with separate large earthfast posts set at average intervals of 1m [895, 1022, 1024, 629]. These defined a circle 8m in diameter. However, a substantial part of the building lay beyond the northern limits of Trench B and its E half was truncated by the later E barmkin wall. Despite this, the surviving

Fig 11 View of Structure 6 post pits (Period 2a) and S side of Structure 14 (Period 2b) from NW.

fragments of the building included an entrance facing SE, with traces of what may possibly have been a porch [883], associated with two successive floor deposits, features [856] and [138].

Immediately inside the house was a setting comprising two pitched stones in an L-shape configuration. This did not appear to have had any structural significance in terms of the house construction, and appeared to represent some sort of working surface or crude table. Finds from inside the building included coarse pottery, animal bones, especially cattle, as well as numerous burnt bones, charcoal and ash.

Group III, Structure 5

This building was the successor to Structure 6 and its construction saw a shift of the building platform to the SE (Figs 9 and 12), as indeed was noted in the case of Structure 1. The building itself was of wall-slot and wall-post construction and had a diameter of 8.5m, centring on an outcrop of weathered bedrock, which showed some signs of direct heat (possibly from a hearth).

Post-holes [182] [831] [836] and [826] were rock-cut, or more specifically were formed by forcing the natural fissuring in the doleritic sill apart, forming slot-like depressions 0.2m deep. Some of these voids [e.g. 182, 826] included roughly rounded pits with packers. This building technique was much more in evidence in Structures 15 and 17 (see below), and was possibly used because of the absence of clay till cover, into which post-holes might otherwise have been excavated.

Burnt and unburnt animal bones were recovered from deposits within the building, along with fragments of coarse pottery.

Paved Threshold [820]

This patch of laid schist slabs lay towards the S side of the building, at the northern limits of the trench. It was roughly rectangular (2.3 × 1.7m) in plan, with a post setting at its NW corner [830], some 0.15m deep. The upper surface of the threshold had sustained considerable wear and some of the thinner slabs had cracked *in situ*.

Pit [892]

A small rounded depression 1m to the W of threshold [820] measured 0.45m in diameter with a depth of 0.18m. Its fill was a mixed charcoal-rich soil with a few stones. The lining of this feature, interpreted as a simple bowl furnace or crucible, was a skin of local clay, discoloured by heat, some 20mm thick.

The Outer Defences, a Palisade?

A rock-cut slot [750] was revealed to the north of the Period 2a structures in Trench H (Fig 9), but had been truncated by the later barmkin wall to the north and east. The size of this feature, its proximity to the northern limits of occupation on the site and its relative isolation all suggested that it represented a perimeter defence, in the form of a palisade.

The feature comprised a straight-sided gully, 4m in length, cut into the bedrock and lying towards the extreme NE corner of the trench. The line of the slot exploited a natural fissure in the bedrock and was traceable for a further 3.5m. The slot was up to 0.5m wide and 0.3m deep, the posts themselves being defined by

Fig 12 View of Structure 14 post pits (Period 2b) cutting across east side of Structure 5 (Period 2a) from SW.

stone packers set in dark humic soil. In all, five post settings were identified in the slot, ranging in diameter from 0.2m to 0.3m [762, 763, 764, 767, 776]. They were set at very close intervals (on average only 0.15–0.2m apart). This may have been a consequence of the limited depth of soil available for supporting the posts, but also implies a 'stockade' type of construction.

PERIOD 2B: THE FORT IN THE EARLY HISTORIC PERIOD, AD *c.*600–*c.*1000 (Figs 8, 13–14)

Drystone Mound and Revetting Wall – Structure 17

A mound lay towards the middle of Trench B, extending the natural summit of the hill to the west and east. The mound was later extended, elevated and then eroded in subsequent building phases from the late Iron Age through to the 16th century. Unfortunately the largely irregular drystone build of the structure prevented any more than limited excavation. This and the periodic alterations that it had sustained meant that much of the detail of its original form and function remained obscure.

The structure (Structure 17, Figs 12 and 14) comprised three elements. The southernmost and most substantial was a roughly rectangular mound of angled and pitched stones of uniform size, which projected from the levelled summit of the hill. The whole structure measured some 7m by 8m. Its upper layer [156] sealed a well-compacted metalled surface [325], which was revetted in turn by a wide drystone wall [223] along its E side.

During Period 2, Structure 17 defined one side of a revetted platform creating a yard area in front of the Group I buildings (Structures 1 and 4). It is clear that wall [223] was never intended to stand to any great height during the occupation of the Group I buildings. Structure 17 was therefore likely to have been of timber and drystone construction, much of the evidence for which would have been removed when the mound was extended in Period 3 (see below). The Period 3 phase of construction was represented by the dumping of rubble [017], which was found to seal patchy deposits covering the irregular surface of [156]. These deposits [088, 089] suggest that [156] was an exposed surface or floor. They contained a variety of material, including bones of cattle, pig, dog and horse along with coarse pottery fragments. This may be interpreted as domestic rubbish, associated with the Period 2 houses.

The metalled surface [325] appears to have been integral to the drystone wall [223] that revetted it. When sectioned it was found to have been laid in successive layers of pitched and flat stones, covering the voids and declivities in the bedrock. The upper surface, where exposed, comprised a mixture of cobbles and patchy paving in the style of the paving noted in the area of the main entrance and in the threshold of Structure 6. The surface also sealed an isolated threshold [821], which lay to the N and E. This apparently belonged to a building similar to Structure 6, whose limits were not identified.

Because the metalled surface levelled the uneven bedrock exposures towards the summit of the hill, it was of variable depth, but was on average some 0.3m thick. Other than bedrock, the surface sealed an orange clay surface [890], which

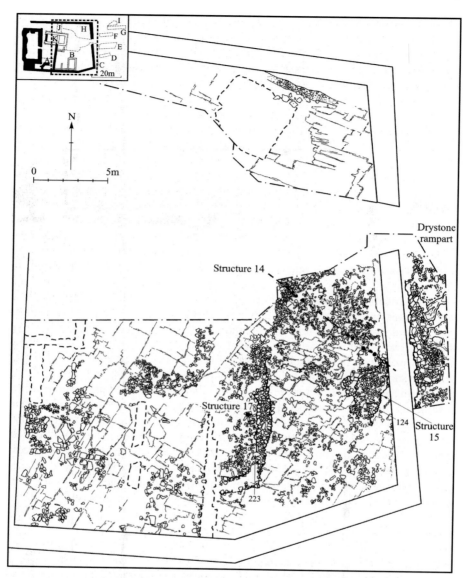

Fig 13 Plan showing Period 2b structures against bedrock surface.

may have been a remanent of the natural till cover, discoloured by the percolation of water through the rocky matrix. Only a small section of this surface was exposed towards the N end of the metalled surface. It was found to have been cut by three pits. One of these was shallow and clay-lined [892], the lining having been fired. Two samples from this context were dated at SURRC by thermoluminescence to 180–730 BC and 380–700 BC respectively. Given their imprecision (due in the main to water penetration), these dates might best be regarded as indicating a period sometime in the Iron Age (see pp. 121–3).

Fig 14 View of Structure 17 (Period 2b) during excavation from N.

Although the function of the pits is unknown, the archaeological evidence suggests that Structure 17 post-dated the earlier Iron Age phase on the site (Period 2a). It appears to have comprised a well-constructed enclosed platform, which may have received a timber building, little trace of which survived. Threshold [821] appeared not to be integral to the [223/325] complex, but did respect the same house site and featured a porch or paved threshold similar to those noted in Structures 4 and 6, the earliest recognisable house forms identified.

Only a few finds were retrieved from features [156] and [325]. They included a shale bracelet fragment (SF 40) and a rubbing or grind stone (SF 39) as well as animal bone and coarse pottery.

The Period 2b Entrance to the Site

Although most of the detail of the primary route into the settlement had been obscured by medieval building works (particularly by the Period 4 E gatehouse), enough evidence survived towards the eastern limits of Trench B to indicate that access into the innermost circuit of the earlier fortification lay between structure Groups II and III. A series of metalled surfaces within a natural gully in the bedrock was revealed, against one edge of which was a deep groove worn either by vehicular traffic or by the backswing of a large, heavy door (Fig 15).

The Period 2b Straight-Sided Buildings (Structures 14 and 15, Figs 10 and 12)

Complete ground plans were identified for two straight-sided buildings and groups of associated features. It was evident that they had been destroyed deliberately. The demolition and spreading of Structure 15 infilled the earlier narrow road into the fort. In view of this and the fact that this building lay between the Group II and III structures, it is possible that it was associated with the defended entrance to the early enclosure. Elaborate gateways are often a feature of such fortifications and indeed some form of gatehouse would be likely on a site of this size and evident importance. In addition, the destruction of Structure 15 appeared to have been contemporary with that of the drystone rampart a few metres to the E. A small spearhead (SF 89) found below the spread remains of this building again suggests an Early Historic date for both events and appears to support the dating of the rampart's destruction by thermoluminescence to c. AD 1000 (see below). The presence of a bone nail-headed pin (SF 36) and sherds of E-ware (SF 42) reinforce this mid 1st-millennium dating.

Structure 15 was characterised by a complex dump of angled, fire-reddened stonework covering a rectangular area, 4.2m by 4m, which sealed extensive charcoal-rich deposits. The latter sealed a few post settings, which were consistent in size and aligned NW to SE, following the natural lie of the bedrock. The posts were of two types: simple earthfast posts with packers, and posts set in localised patches of crude paving.

The likeliest interpretation of this group of features is that they represent a collapsed timber and stone structure. It was ablaze when demolished, and once the superstructure had collapsed, the still smouldering timbers were sealed by the collapse of low drystone walls. This sequence gave rise to a stony crust over the

Fig 15 View of Period 2b entrance showing worn bedrock from W.

deep charcoal spreads, as in all probability combustion was maintained for some time after the building was completely levelled.

The material sealing this assemblage consisted of three spreads of variously heat-affected deposits, represented by features [079], [124] and [326]. The highly organic quality of these deposits indicated the former presence of turf. This overlay stonier and more compacted levels, representing the collapsed debris within the entranceway. A bone peg (SF 81) and a shale loomweight (SF 80) from the occupation horizon [326] were trapped beneath the collapsed and spread debris itself [124] and the secondary post-demolition burnt horizon [079]. All the evidence points to a sudden and wholesale destruction by fire to a degree only seen elsewhere on the vitrified rampart fragment to the E (see below).

The structural debris (particularly [124]) was very extensive (Fig 12), but the structure(s) from which it was derived was not. The disposition of the debris and the probability that it had not moved far from its source, together with the fact that it sealed a roadway sequence, suggests that Structure 15 was not a stand-alone building, but represented some form of passage or entranceway. Indeed, it seems likely to have represented a defended entrance or gateway. The roadway itself, worn into a natural gully in the bedrock and much repaired, reflected the most intensively used thoroughfare of all those encountered in the fort. It was aligned SE to NW and appeared to curve toward the centre of the fort (as defined by the line of the vitrified rampart) from the SE; before turning towards the nucleus of the fort, it appeared to pass in front of the drystone rampart.

A line of posts associated with a low stone kerb or revetting wall (Structure 14, Fig 11) was identified on the same alignment as Structure 15. In addition, a second series of slighter post settings lay parallel to the main series. Immediately S of these post settings evidence was revealed of another parallel line. It may be that the latter group of posts was associated with the enlargement of Structure 15, rather than forming part of Structure 14, as it lay some 5m from the northern series of kerb posts; it was also mostly rock-cut, or more accurately formed by the enlargement of natural fissures in the bedrock. It is probable that the rock-cut line was associated with the two others identified in Period 2, though it is not clear whether they represented a hall-like building or some sort of stockade.

These groups of features post-dated both Structures 5 and 6 but were so disturbed as to prevent all but the most general structural associations. However, if they represented a separate building rather than fence lines, it may be that they formed part of the later, pre-medieval domestic structures, and are the remains of a hall-like building. Unfortunately, the later medieval access from the E, particularly the stone ramps, which may indeed be the heaped remnants of dwarf stone walls from such a hall, destroyed much of the earlier archaeology.

The Period 2b Defences – The Vitrified Rampart

Only two recognisable fragments of the once very extensive defences of the Period 2 fortification were revealed, and these were isolated from one another. Consequently their relative dating was impossible to establish, but given that the terraced nature of the hill determined the lines of the defensive circuits, the two fragments could well indicate inner and outer wall lines.

In Trench C, a section of vitrified masonry was identified, truncated to the south by later wall lines (Figs 16 and 17). It lay immediately east of the Period 6 E barmkin wall, the erection of which damaged it slightly; indeed, the 15th-century builders appear to have robbed it extensively for rubble to use in their wall. Despite this, the feature was still very impressive and both its timber-laced construction and the evidence of the firing process involved in its vitrification were clearly visible.

Only the inner face of the vitrified rampart was excavated. It appears to have been *c*. 4m thick at its base, but only the lowest part of it survived. As far as can be determined it was built on a terrace towards the break of slope on the E side of the hill's summit. It seems to have had a steeply battered external face, which extended the natural profile of the hill. Some 8.5m of the inner face of the wall were revealed in Trench C. It comprised a series of large fire-reddened and cracked natural boulders, only one course high, laid directly on to the ground rather than in a foundation trench. In all, about half of the full width of the wall's base was revealed. This was made up almost exclusively of dumped, locally quarried angular dolerite fragments. This material displayed the progressive degrees of heat encountered within the wall fabric, from cracking and discolouration to the fusing of individual stones, culminating in the total melting of the rock. The wall-core had sustained the highest temperatures. This gradation of the heat-affected areas and the presence within this material of beam slots, two horizontal and one vertical, conforms to the 'classic' structure of vitrified ramparts. A provisional date of *c*. AD 1000 for the firing obtained by thermoluminescence (Strickertson *et al.* 1988) suggests an early historic to early medieval date for this destruction of the site's defences.

The process of vitrifaction on the drystone rampart had been progressive, with the heat source coming from the top and sides of the structure. It is not certain whether the beam slots themselves acted as flues within the fabric of the wall, but it is noteworthy that at Dundonald the slots have retained their outline within or near to molten material and were not heavily distorted. It is clear however that as the stonework was progressively heated, the structure started to give way from the outer face, which fell to the east down the hill. Once this process was underway and the wall was collapsing, the molten wall core simply flowed down to the east over the less well-fired lower courses of the wall, as was found in Trench C.

The alignments of the beam slots and of the partially surviving the inner wall-face suggest that the rampart did not follow exactly the line of the later barmkin wall, apparently because it was aligned to take account of the jointing of the bed-rock. The S end of the rampart was marked by a straight edge with fire-reddened stones, suggesting a deliberate termination rather than a later truncation. Although the construction of the medieval barmkin removed any stratigraphic links between the vitrified rampart and the fortified entrance identified in or around Structure 15, it is likely that the S end of the rampart was associated in some way with a gate and ancillary structures.

The excavated fragment of vitrified rampart indicated that most of the wall core became effectively molten. Consequently it must have sustained heat for a considerable period, probably in excess of 24 hours. The evidence also suggests that the heat was applied from the outside, where one would expect most of the

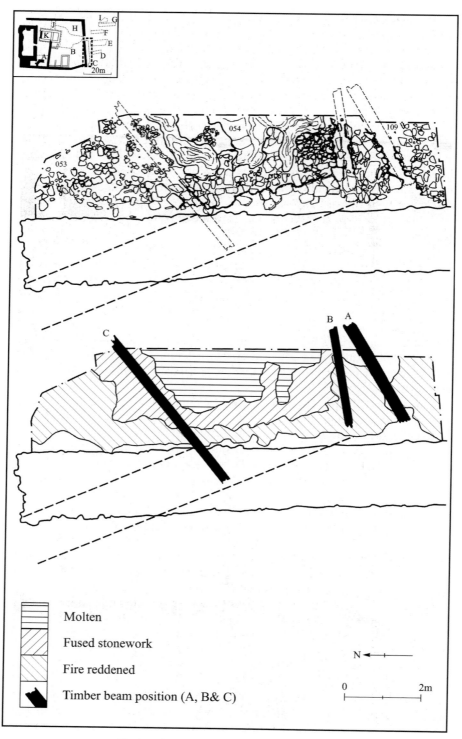

Fig 16 Plan of vitrified rampart (Period 2b).

Fig 17 View of Period 2b vitrified rampart (under ranging rods) adjacent to barmkin wall (Period 5), from N.

combustion to have occurred, in the presence of oxygen; however, it was trans-
ferred to the wall core, creating there temperatures very much higher than on the
wall surface. The probability is that the timber lacing would have assisted in this
process, but it is unlikely that the phenomenon of vitrifaction on this scale was the
accident of an attack on the site. Rather the evidence implies the deliberate
systematic destruction of the rampart or key parts of it, perhaps after the site had
been captured.

As in the case of Structure 15, it is very difficult to establish whether all or
only some of the structures in the inner part of the fort were standing at the same
time as the rampart. Despite the fact that the full circuit of the rampart was far from
clear, it certainly appeared that Structure 6 had either been built into its inner face
or pre-dated it. There was also some evidence to suggest that Structures 14 and 15
represented a shift away from round buildings to straight-sided ones, perhaps with
the final enhancement of Structure 17 occurring at this time.

PERIOD 3: *c*. 1000–*c*. 1241 (Figs 8, 18–19)

Structure 16a, A Timber Hall

Structure 16a (Figs 18 and 19) was built of timber over a sub-rectangular mound.
The mound was delineated at its E and S sides by the remains of the Period 2 'hall'
(Structure 17) and was formed by creating a level platform up to the height of the
natural summit of the castle hill. Stratified deposits therefore survived best to the
south, where the ground was levelled up, making it possible to distinguish posts
from different phases.

Like its Period 2 predecessor, the structure was aligned N-S and was of slight
construction, as evinced by the small size of the posts defining it. The most
substantial element of the structure was its building platform [017], which was
constructed of angular fragments of local dolerite. The mound was revetted on
the east with several pitched stones, creating a step 0.30m high. Significantly it
contained no ashlar or mortared rubble, thus confirming its pre-Period 4 date. It
may be that elements of the Period 2 hall, notably walls [223] and [224], were
demolished and spread to form the platform.

Evidence for the superstructure consisted of voids within the random
stonework of feature [017]. The posts that evidently once sat in them may well
have had the mound built around them, as the voids did not always appear to be
intrusive features. This aspect of the construction and the generally voided nature
of the mound inevitably made the identification of post-holes difficult. However,
differences in alignment and construction allowed two series of post settings to be
distinguished. These appear to have related to two structures, here designated 16a
and 16b.

Once the components of Structure 16a were recognised, the plan of an early
hall-like building emerged. The regularity of feature [017] and the discovery of
evenly spaced posts suggested that the building was of timber construction. In all,
twelve post-settings were identified. These defined the E, S and W walls of a sub-
rectangular building. A series of similar settings inside the building may relate to

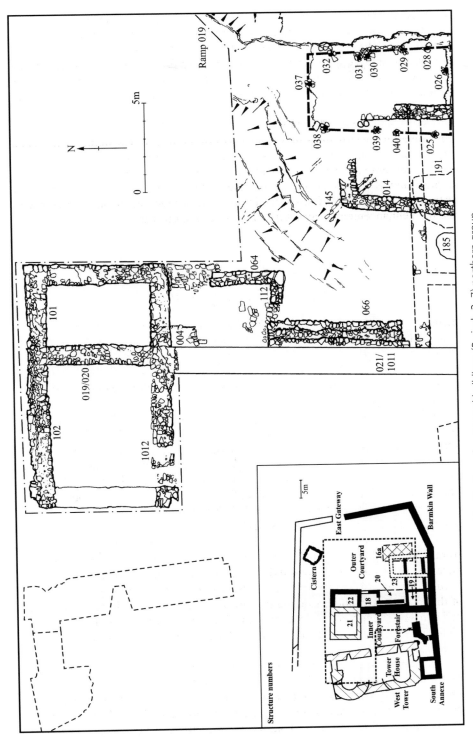

Fig 18 Plan of excavated buildings (Periods 2–7) northern group.

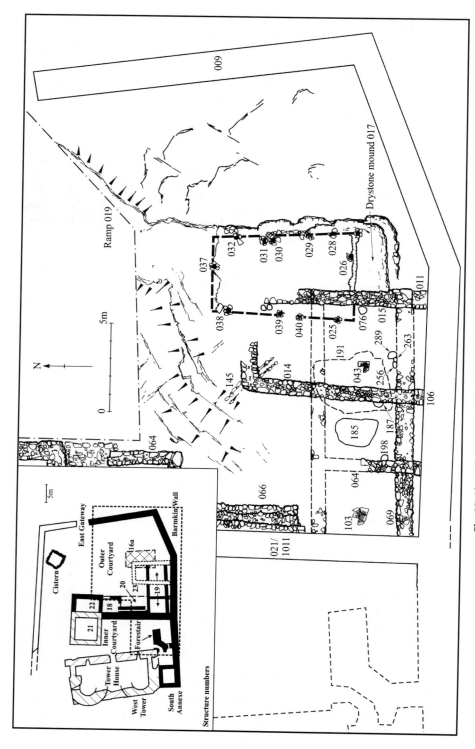

Fig 19 Plan of excavated buildings (Periods 2–7) southern group.

the subdivision of the interior or to supports for the roof, or both. The spacing and size of the wall-posts suggest that the walls played little or no part in supporting the roof. They were probably infilled with wattle or turf, but there was no evidence of timber shuttering (e.g. nails) or stonework.

From the likely position of a door in the W wall of the hall, a drain [145] ran NW for a distance of some 3m. It followed a natural fissure in the bedrock and was capped crudely with flat stones. Its location and method of construction suggests that it would have been associated with Structure 16a, perhaps serving to carry away both domestic waste and rainwater.

A drystone ramp [019] appears to have given access to building platform [017] from the E, following one of the regular terraces or steps in the bedrock (Figs 18 and 19). The feature itself was up to 4m wide and merged with the northern end of [017]. As with [017], the stony matrix of the ramp is likely to have had a level walking surface if only of trampled earth. However, due to the fact that post-abandonment weathering, worm action and root penetration were so extreme, much of the actual surface of the ramp had simply eroded away.

Taken together, all the evidence suggests that there was a timber building aligned N–S measuring 5.3m by 2.8m, which was approached from the E but was probably entered on the W. The absence of any evidence for a hearth may signify a non-residential function.

The 16b Group of Features

A further building was associated with 16a. This was of dwarf stone-wall construction, a technique which entailed the embedding of wall posts within the thickness of crude unbonded stonework. In several cases the posts penetrated the natural clay till below; but, because of the extent of later occupation of this site, many of the drystone alignments had been robbed or had shifted. The hearth [043] identified in Structure 19 (Period 6) may well have originated in this period, as it formed a focus for the various building plans identified. The most obvious post settings were traced within short sections of drystone walling [e.g. 076, 104], defined by pitched settings, which formed part of the E wall but were later built over by Structure 23 (Period 7). Elsewhere post settings emerged beneath later walls and floors from Period 6 occupation [e.g. 187, 198].

The series of possible floors identified with Structure 16b overlay cleaner levelling or infilling deposits within fissures in the bedrock and over the remains of Period 2 structures. A series of lensate horizons were found within the levelling deposits, presumably reflecting continuing repair and maintenance of the interior of Structure 16b.

Structure 16b was further evinced by patches of levelling and flooring [185, 191], which defined the W end and central areas of the building. These may indicate two separate rooms within an overall structure up to 7.5m long. There is evidence that some posts were replaced or relocated slightly: post [263], for instance, appeared to have been replaced by [256], while the adjacent [289], a larger and more massive setting, may well have been integral to the roof support and less easily replaced. Decorated glass and pottery found within primary fills of feature [289] confirmed a medieval date, but represented almost one hundred years of usage. The plan of the building and its internal subdivision suggest a possible interpretation as a hall and chamber, or solar.

The 'Motte'

An artificial mound of earth, clay and rubble, exposed in the construction and stone-robbing trenches around the N tower of the later Period 4 E gatehouse, lay against the NE flank of the Castle Hill and occupied an area outwith the assumed line of the natural defences of Periods 1 and 2 (Figs 8 and 20). This earthwork extended the profile of the rocky, terraced outcrop beyond the natural break in slope, thereby creating a platform.

The platform was later cut by the foundations for the N tower of the E gatehouse (Period 4) and by a stone-robbing trench [943] (from Period 5), which was partially excavated in Trench I. The sides of this trench showed the platform to have had a boulder and clay base, sealed by an earthen deposit [947], containing a few stones. The drystone boulder and clay platform [950, 951] seems to have acted both as a base and as a regular revetment for the earthwork. The later construction of the gatehouse tower had obscured the true profile and height of the earthwork, but surviving sections of its basal profile suggested a steep-sided structure.

Ceramic sherds found in the earthwork confirmed its medieval origins. Although it was only exposed in a single trench (Trench I), it is postulated that this platform represents the truncated remains of a motte. Such a motte would have been appended to what remained of the early defensive circuit and could have been sited in order to overlook the natural approaches to the hill summit from the east. Surveys of the hill's topography suggest that the surviving parts of the earthwork were represented by the 53m contour to the east of the Period 4 N tower base (Fig 8). It is also tempting to see the creation of the massive level terrace (presently unexcavated) that forms the northern half of the Period 4 castle area as in part formed from material recycled from the motte; as it stood adjacent to the terrace it would have been redundant in the new Period 4 layout.

PERIOD 4: c. 1241–c. 1300 (Figs 8, 20–25)

During the second half of the 13th century, the castle was rebuilt in stone to a new design, which on the evidence of the excavations was both elaborate and substantial. As the Period 4 castle seems never to have been completed and what was built survived only in a very damaged state, it is difficult to make a full assessment of the structure that was planned. This period of building and occupation ended with the partial destruction of what had been built, possibly as a consequence of siege. However, some stone from the building seems to have been used subsequently in the creation of the late 14th-century tower-house (Period 6, see below).

The Period 4 castle was a fortress of *enceinte*; the interior was left virtually empty, which explains why evidence for earlier occupation survived relatively undisturbed beneath the later courtyard deposits. It took the form of a kite-shaped enclosure with two massive twin-towered gatehouses placed at the diametrically

Fig 20 View from tower showing the platform for Structure 16a (Period 3) and outer courtyard (Period 5) from W.

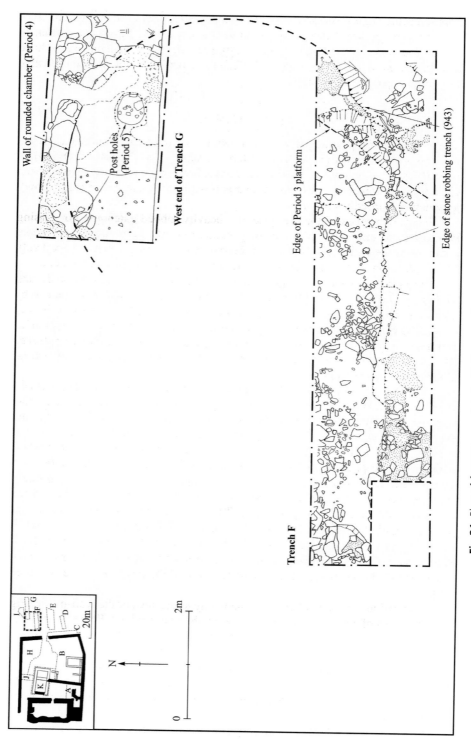

Fig 21 Plan of features associated with N tower of E gatehouse (Period 4).

Wall of rounded chamber (Period 4)

Post holes (Period 5)

West end of Trench G

Edge of Period 3 platform

Edge of stone robbing trench (943)

Trench F

2m

0

N

20m

G
F
E
D
C
B
H
J
K
A

opposed acute angles. As in the earlier fort and castle, it seems likely that the E of these was the principal gate, though the W one appears to have been similar in design. It is also likely that the two other, obtuse angles of the enceinte would have been protected by projecting towers of some kind, but it has not yet been possible to examine them by excavation.

The East Gatehouse

The existence of this structure was unknown before the excavation began. However, because its investigation was limited to a series of trial trenches (D–F, I) its overall form and extent have had to be extrapolated from evidence derived from discontinuous trenches and from comparison with the W gatehouse (see below), to which it is broadly similar.

Excavation revealed the presence of a heavily robbed gatehouse comprising two towers on either side of a narrow passage, towards the E edge of the upper contours of the castle hill. Neither of the two towers was excavated completely and the N tower was significantly more reduced than its southern counterpart.

The entrance passage of the gatehouse appears to have been 4m wide and 12m long, and was lined by two walls of lime-mortared ashlar. It was flanked by guard chambers, the outward faces of which were rounded, both externally and internally, while the rear wall facing the courtyard appears to have been straight. From the outside the gatehouse would have given the impression of an entrance flanked by rounded towers, though the towers would in fact each have had an elongated D-shape on plan.

Only the southern tower of the gatehouse was investigated in any detail. It was exposed in Trench E (Figs 22–23) over one season of excavation, which was intended primarily to confirm the date and function of the eastern defences to the site. The excavation revealed two separate chambers within the S tower. To the east was a well within a small, almost square room (Fig 24). Five courses of ashlar lining survived at the top of the well shaft (Fig 25). Below this, the lining was constructed of unmortared, roughly dressed whin blocks. Since it is most likely that the well was fissure-fed, the change in construction probably reflected the point at which bedrock was penetrated. The shaft was cleared only to a depth of 1.85m, slightly below the level of water seepage. It was noted that the N and W walls of the well-house were bonded into the core of the shaft but that the E wall appeared to be a later replacement. It is possible therefore that the room may have been D-shaped originally although too little of the tower was revealed to be certain.

A second internal chamber lay immediately to the west of the well-house (Fig 21) and traces of a possible doorway between the two survived. Some 0.5m of fill was removed from the W chamber down to a flagged floor. Most of the outer face of the main structure proved to have been robbed. To the W a short stretch of whin facing survived to three courses. No facing survived on the N edge of the structure. In the NE corner of the trench a deposit of rubble, mortar and fragments of ashlar, 1.5m deep, was removed to expose four courses of white sandstone curving to the S and with a steep batter.

A short stretch of Period 4 masonry uncovered towards the S end of Trench C

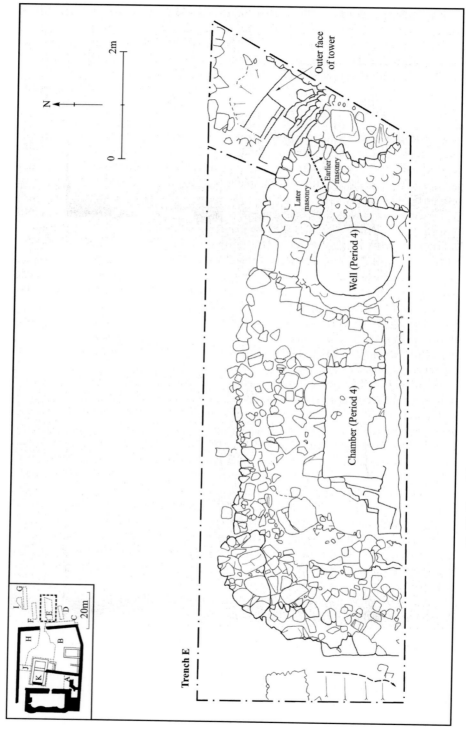

Fig 22 Plan of features associated with S tower of E gatehouse (Period 4).

Fig 23 View from E of S tower of the E gatehouse (Period 4) under excavation.

Fig 24 View from N of the outer face of the S tower of the E gatehouse (Period 4).

Fig 25 View from W of the well in the S tower of the E gatehouse (Period 4).

appears to have been laid out parallel to the curtain wall, which ran SW from the S face of the gatehouse's southern tower. To judge from its build, the masonry appears to have represented the inner wall of a building or range constructed against the inside face of the curtain wall.

Parts of the N tower were excavated in 1988 and evidence of a lime-mortared structure with one surviving inner chamber was retrieved (Fig 20). The chamber lay at the E end of the tower and was circular or sub-circular in plan (up to 4.8m in diameter). The outer walls of the tower did not survive but were found to have been constructed in a foundation trench.

The West Gatehouse (Figs 8 and 26)

It had long been suspected that the great tower of Dundonald Castle had been built over the remains of a demolished or perhaps unfinished two-towered gatehouse of late 13th-century type (Simpson 1950, 11–14; Cruden 1981, 121; cf. MacGibbon and Ross 1887-92, I, 168-9). This now appears to be confirmed both by the discovery of a second gatehouse of the same type occupying a corresponding position on the E side of the hill and by close examination of the tower's foundations and base.

Inside the tower's basement the outline of the earlier gatehouse is clearly recognisable. The lower parts of the NW and SW corners, for instance, incorporate the curved interior faces of two rounded towers, each about 4.5m across internally. If we assume that the E wall of the tower corresponded to the E wall of the gatehouse, the two guard chambers inside the towers would have been some 8m from east to west. The curved walling survived to a height of 2.5m in the NW corner and over 3m in the SW. Above this level the builders of the later tower drew in the walls to a more regular quadrangular plan by spanning the curved angles with segmental arches. The walls that flanked the gate passage were apparently demolished when the 14th-century tower-house was built, and although traces of the abutments of two crosswalls may still be observed on the east and west walls, these appear to relate to a pend within the basement of the later tower-house, rather than to the passage in the original gatehouse (see below). The original pend seems likely to have been about 4m wide and the walls separating it from the guard chambers about 2.5–3m.

Externally the evidence for the gatehouse may be seen most clearly at the base of the west wall. At the N end, part of the ashlar facing the curved external *talus* of the tower appears to survive *in situ*, though it is also possible that this simply represents a 14th-century attempt at tidying up what would otherwise have been a somewhat irregular masonry projection. The S tower also seems to have projected forward from the line of the present wall, though not as much as the N one. Four to five metres above ground level, however, the wall straightens out, the tops of the two projections being marked by a chamfered ashlar string course. Although in the 1940s Simpson claimed to have been able to observe the outlines of the inner and outer gates in the tower's east and west walls respectively, robbed of their jambs and voussoirs and then walled-up (1950: 11–12), his interpretation is not supported by the evidence visible today. In part this may be due to the extensive consolidation that the tower has undergone in the intervening period; but

Fig 26 View from W of the S tower of the E gatehouse (Period 4).

it also seems doubtful whether the original gatehouse's outer arch would have been set as far forward as the present tower-house's W wall or that the gatehouse survived to a sufficient height to have preserved any trace of the arch.

Excavation inside the pit prison below the Period 5 annexe to the tower also revealed at the base of the tower's S wall the curving SW face of the gatehouse's south tower. This was represented by two courses of mortared angular dolerite blocks, which curved out from the NW corner of the chamber and continued for 1.5m. This short length of masonry was built directly over the natural bedrock outcrop and clay till and was sealed by the pit prison's N wall.

The reason for building a W gatehouse in Period 4 is not immediately obvious, given that the E gatehouse lay on the usual route into the site used in all previous periods. A conspicuous earthwork on the W side of the castle hill might possibly relate to Period 4, or even Period 3; but whatever the case, this would have done little to facilitate access on to the hill from the west on a scale appropriate to so massive a gatehouse. It seems possible therefore that construction of the W gatehouse was due as much to a desire for symmetry as to any practical defensive requirements.

PERIOD 5: AD c. 1300–c. 1371 (Figs 8, 20–21, 28)

The E gatehouse appears to have been slighted in antiquity and partially refurbished in timber prior to its final demolition and the robbing of its stones. Similar sequences were also revealed in Trenches E and J, in the courtyard area of the castle. Although the dating of these events was complicated by the late medieval robbing the findings in both towers of the gatehouse were broadly consistent

The South Tower of the East Gatehouse

The partial demolition of the S tower was reflected by clear attempts to dismantle the outer face. It was noted that the exposed surviving ashlar blocks of the outer facing of the S tower were sealed by a deep horizon, possibly a turf line or ground surface. This dense soil accumulation [522] had been cut into in order to prize out facing slabs from the tower, some of which were still *in situ* but displaced.

Some of the walls of this partially damaged tower were then rebuilt and may then have been augmented with timberwork. The accumulated soil (522) was sealed by deposits reflecting the partial reconstruction of a square well-house over the circular well-shaft in the E chamber (see above). The rebuilding of the well-house was reflected by its E wall [521], which was found to be of later construction than the other walls

Accumulated rubble over and within the W chamber blocked the door into the well-house, and the absence of rubble within the well-house itself suggested that the latter continued in use after the demolition of at least the W chamber, if not the collapse of the whole gatehouse.

The entire sequence was then sealed by a deposit of fire-derived debris, including burnt clay and charred wood. This deposit reflected a separate period of damage which postdated the initial destruction of the tower. This suggests that the

Fig 27 View from W of NW corner of the Castle showing remains of N tower of
W gatehouse embedded in later tower house (Period 6).

timberwork was contemporary with the refurbishment of parts of the damaged
gatehouse.

Landscaping in Period 5 saw the spreading of this burnt horizon so that its
depth and relationship to remains of structures surviving *in situ* was impossible to
determine. The cut timber, daub and cob all seem to have come from demolished
timber structures. However, the absence of heat-affected masonry from both

towers of the gatehouse suggests that the focus of the fire that had consumed these structures was elsewhere, albeit presumably close enough to allow the resulting debris to cover the gatehouse's robbed-out remains. One possibility is that the debris came from a timber superstructure that had been built over the unfinished or partially dismantled masonry base of the gatehouse.

Once the refurbished tower was finally burnt down the remains were spread and levelled.

The North Tower of the East Gatehouse

In the N tower, the robbing in Period 5 was considerably more extensive than in its S counterpart. It resulted in the wholesale removal of the external facing stones, leaving only the mortar core.

The rebuilding in timber was reflected by two post settings cut into the floor of the chamber, which had in turn been levelled up. The post-holes suggest continued repair and usage of the W chamber, prior to the final destruction of the tower. The reuse of parts of the damaged gatehouse is also suggested by evidence surviving in the rounded room in the N tower. Here a mortar floor was laid over a deliberate infilling, after the primary structure had been demolished to a height of only three courses of ashlar facing.

The timberwork over the reduced remains of the N tower was apparently burnt down. Within the partially exposed rounded chamber (assumed to be the W chamber, the E chamber having now been totally removed) further evidence was found of the dumping of fire-derived material directly over occupation levels (Fig 28). The extent of the burning was indicated by its presence over the W chamber of the N gatehouse tower, where daub and nails were found even in the topsoil, alongside green-glaze reduced ware pottery from the Period 6 robbing and levelling phases. Charcoal and daub were found in increasing abundance at depths more than 0.15m below the present ground surface. Tipped deposits were identified over the earliest burnt deposits, which included quite large timber fragments, some up to 0.30m in length.

Three large carbonised timbers (one possibly a joist or beam), which appeared to have been burnt *in situ* and were associated with large quantities of burnt and baked daub or cob, were found overlying the secondary floor. At least 50 iron nails were associated with this deposit, although they were not physically attached to either the timber or the daub. A similar deposit of daub, nails and large fragments of carbonised dressed timbers was noted in the western chamber of the S tower, overlying displaced elements of the inner facing. The presence of these two similar horizons within discrete structures appears to indicate the temporary refurbishment – or completion – of the outer defences in timber, prior to their final destruction. The presence of daub or cob with the timbers and nails suggests that these are the remains of a free-standing timber structure and not simply the burnt debris of destroyed floors or roofing timbers.

At some point after the destruction of the timber structure over the N tower a large robber pit was dug, truncating the timbers and removing the E edge of the surviving rounded stone-built chamber. The eastern edge of this pit cut a deposit of clean mortar with occasional stone inclusions, over 1m deep. Initially this horizon was assumed to be demolition material that had collapsed down the hill-

Fig 28 Burnt timber from refurbishment of N tower (Period 5) of E gate house *in situ*.

side, but its relationship to the robbing suggested the more probable explanation that it was wall-core surviving *in situ*. The subsequent infilling of the pit was characterised by successive horizons of burnt material mixed with charcoal and nails, which may be interpreted as the disposal of contemporary surface material. This would suggest that deliberate levelling of the site took place not long after the destructive event.

No dateable material was recovered from the general demolition horizon, which extended across the interior of the S tower as well as over the robbed walls. However, the upper surface featured a cut, which appeared to relate to the clearance of rubble to provide access to the barmkin entrance (Period 6). The fill of the cut produced a number of sherds of medieval pottery, many of which appeared to be from one vessel. Similar sherds were recovered from the top fill of the well-shaft.

A final deposit with significant evidence of burnt timber and clay was found across both robbed gatehouse towers.

A deposit of mortar and rubble in the upper fill of the shaft may relate to the final demolition of the west chamber. Three bone-handled knives or leather working implements were found as a group within this material and appear to represent a casual loss (see pp. 101–3, SF 75).

A tentative historical sequence may be proposed for the archaeological evidence for destruction, followed by repair and again by destruction. The first destruction, possibly affecting the western gatehouse as well as its eastern counterpart, may perhaps have represented the slighting of Dundonald's defences carried out during the Wars of Independence. Following this the castle would have been refurbished. The presence of daub together with the burnt timberwork noted in both towers of the E gatehouse, however, suggests that the rebuilding was carried out in timber over what remained of its masonry base. The practice of using timber to repair masonry defences is documented near by during the Wars of Independence; in May 1302 Edward I instructed Master James of St George to complete in timber the construction of the gate and towers at Linlithgow that had already been begun in stone (Brown, Colvin and Taylor 1963, 412–15; Taylor 1950, 449–51; 1984). At Dundonald, the timber refurbishment would then have been finally destroyed by a conflagration, which produced the burnt deposits overlying the site of the E gatehouse. A possible historical interpretation for this sequence of events is proposed in the discussion section (see pp. 137–8).

PERIOD 6: *c*. 1371–*c*. 1449/50 (Fig 8)

An extensive new building campaign took place at Dundonald towards the end of the 14th century. Although much of the stone used in this work was derived from the earlier castle and its principal element, a lofty tower-house, was constructed over the remains of the earlier western gatehouse, the character of the new building was quite different to that which it replaced. This period saw Dundonald rebuilt as a standard Scottish baronial house of the tower-and-barmkin type. The initiator of the work was almost certainly King Robert II (1371–90), for whom the castle was to become a favourite residence and whose association with it is evidenced by a series of heraldic devices set into the W face of the tower.

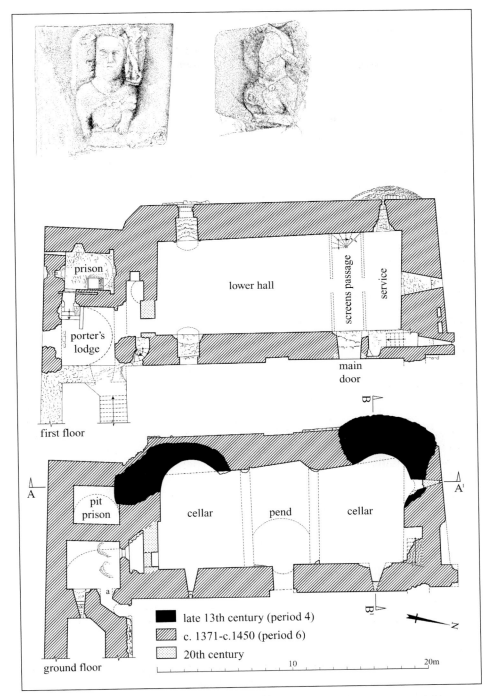

Fig 29 Plans of the tower house at ground and first floors (© Crown copyright, reproduced courtesy of Historic Scotland RCAHMS). Inset shows detail of two decorated corbels flanking the SW window in the lower hall (drawing by Howard Mason).

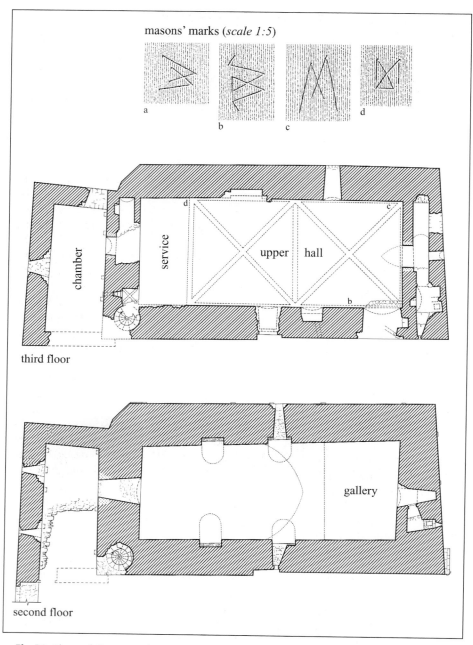

masons' marks (*scale 1:5*)

a   b   c   d

third floor

chamber   service   upper   hall

second floor

gallery

Fig 30 Plans of the tower house at second and third floors with detail of masons marks
on the ribs of the upper hall's vault (© Crown copyright, reproduced courtesy of
RCAHMS).

The Tower-house (Figs 29–40)

The tower-house is a large rectangular structure measuring 24m N–S by 12m E–W with walls 2.3–3.3m thick. The SW corner is chamfered off, while at the E end of the N wall a plain buttress projects, extending two-thirds of the way up the wall. The tower now stands to a maximum height of 19m, but would originally have been at least another 5m higher. Internally it consisted of two barrel-vaulted halls set over a timber-ceiled basement. Above the upper vault there may also have been a timber-roofed garret, enclosed by the wall-walk and containing chambers; but no evidence now survives to indicate how the tower was roofed.

The tower-house is built principally of locally quarried whinstone, with lighter grey or yellow sandstone used for the quoins and dressed work. Pieces of sandstone from the earlier castle are also re-employed randomly in the construction, enriching the texture of its otherwise rather bleak and forbidding appearance (cf. Simpson 1950: 4-5). The surface of the bedrock appears to fall away towards the north-western part of the tower; this may partly explain why the builders chose to retain the rounded base of the northern tower to provide some reinforcement, although some severe vertical cracks visible in the western façade indicate that they were not entirely successful.

The most striking features of the western façade (Figs 31 and 32) are the truncated bases of the two rounded towers from the Period 4 gatehouse (see above). Of these the northern tower projects somewhat more than the southern and still retains some of its ashlar facing. It is possible that in Period 6, as in Period 4, these flanked an entrance to the castle; however, the evidence displayed by the present blocking wall between them is equivocal and will be discussed more fully below. Some 4–5m above ground level a chamfered string course marks the line at which wall-construction was brought back to a regular vertical plane, though at the NW angle this was only achieved by carrying the quoins forward on two roll-moulded corbel courses. The level corresponding to the first floor features three openings: a lintelled slit to the left, a wider window with a pointed-arched head to the right, and another slit with robbed surrounds at a higher level in the centre.

The division between the first and second floors is marked on the W façade by a row of heraldic devices carved on sandstone panels. These comprise heater-shaped shields with armorial bearings, which are identified by W. Douglas Simpson from left to right as follows:

(1) The Lion rampant of Scotland, within the royal tressure, the shield being suspended by a guige or strap from a tree, in the manner of a challenge.
(2) The fess chequy of the Stewarts, the shield hung from a tree by a guige.
(3) The lion rampant and royal tressure.
(4) A weathered shield, hung by a guige. In a favourable light, the charge can be seen to be paly of six. It is therefore that of the ancient Earls of Fife, and must commemorate the marriage of Isabella, Countess of Fife, with Walter, son of King Robert II.
(5) The chevron of Carrick, the shield being hung from a tree by a guige. (Simpson 1950, 13–14) (Fig 33).

The bearing on the fourth shield is now even less discernible than when Simpson

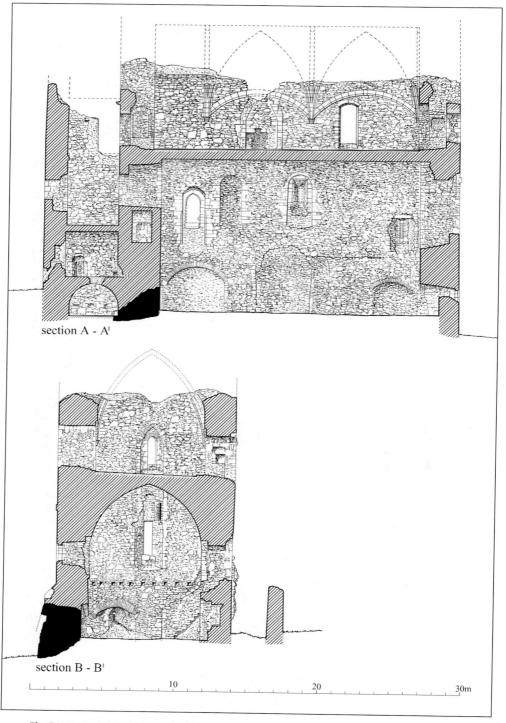

section A - A¹

section B - B¹

10   20   30m

Fig 31 N–S and E–W sections and internal elevations of tower house, looking W and N respectively (© Crown copyright, reproduced courtesy of RCAHMS).

Fig 32 View of W façade of the tower house (Period 6) showing bevelled SW corner and position of heraldic plaques.

recorded it. Below the fifth and running into the chamfered corner of the tower is a longer panel bearing two lions opposed passant gardant, their tails curled down between their hind legs and up over their backs (Fig 34). On the chamfered face at the same level is a much-worn human head.

Another two shields survive at the same level on the N side of the tower, one in the centre and one to the right; but their heraldic designs are no longer discernible. Another two human heads also project from near the top of the N and E sides of the buttress at the NE corner (Fig 29). The E and S façades, however, are undecorated. The window openings have almost all lost their heads; but although the various campaigns of consolidation which the castle has experienced over the last two centuries has resulted in some of them being restored with rounded-arched heads, most would seem originally to have been lintelled or pointed-arched.

The Basement

The basement is irregular in plan, incorporating the remains of the earlier Period 4 gatehouse (see above). It is entered from the east through a door in the centre of the wall facing the courtyard. The head of the door is lost and its original character is difficult to determine. It is set back some 0.25–0.50m in a recess 2m wide which continues vertically to the present wall-head. This would probably at one time have been provided with a machicolation at wall-head level to give some protection to the door below.

Inside the basement, no trace now remains of the inner walls of the towers that formed the sides of the gate-passage. However, looking at the inside face of the door in the 1940s, Simpson was able to observe:

> The present arched door here is placed in the middle of a conspicuous infilling, and the irregular jointing on both sides where the dressed jambs of the original rear-portal have been withdrawn is unmistakable. Above the present door, a rough irregular chase or slot, in the form of a segmental arch, shows where the vaulting of the trance has been pulled out. The height of the crown of the vault was about 12 feet [3.66m]. (1950, 12)

The consolidation work undertaken on the tower in recent years makes these features difficult to identify and interpret. While Simpson may be correct however in relating some of them to the Period 4 gatehouse, given that the tower's E wall appears to built over the remains of the E wall of the earlier gatehouse, the evidence that he presents for a corresponding blocked opening in the W wall of the tower is more questionable. On the outer face of the W wall the curved bases of the two towers that flanked the Period 4 gate were left *in situ* and the pend between them was blocked with masonry. According to Simpson, this blocking preserved the trace of the original outer portal:

> All the dressed stones of its jambs and arch were taken out when the entry was blocked: but part of the overhanging masonry, showing the rough irregular curving profile left by the tails of the voussoirs when these were torn out, remains to tell of the vanished portal.

Inside the keep, the infilling of the entry is equally distinct, with the

Fig 33 Detailed view of plaque showing chevron of Carrick within the W façade of tower house (Period 6).

Fig 34 Detailed view of two lions 'passant' at S end of W façade of tower house (Period 6).

overhanging original masonry above. On the north side of it, there is still to be seen the stub or tusking of a massive party-wall, about 4 feet [1.22m] thick, crossing the gatehouse so as to form the north side of the trance. On the south side, a conspicuous joint in the masonry marks the position of the corresponding party-wall, the corework of which is evident, though this wall has been closed off flush. This remnant defines the limit of the infilled work where once the gate-arch stood and gives us a width of some 9 feet [2.75m] for the trance. (1950, 11–12)

Although no trace of an external portal is now in evidence, the stubs of the internal walls defining a pend or trance may still be observed in both the E wall and the W. These walls would have been too slight to have formed part of the Period 4 gatehouse, whose outer portal should in any case have been more deeply recessed between the flanking towers. It seems much more probable therefore that these cross walls belonged to the Period 6 tower-house. One of their functions would evidently have been to support the timber first floor, evidence of which survives in a row of joist pockets in the N wall, 3.8m above floor level. If we assume that the other ends of these joists were supported by the northern of the two crosswalls, the span involved would have been a little under 7m. A similar arrangement may also be envisaged for the southern compartment. Quite possibly, as Simpson infers, the transe between the crosswalls was covered by a segmental barrel-vault. No doubt there would have been doors in the crosswalls linking the pend with the northern and southern compartments of the basement. However, if another function of the transe was to give access to the portal that Simpson claimed to have detected in the W side of the tower, such an opening (if it existed) must also have related to the Period 6 tower-house rather than to the Period 4 gatehouse. Indeed, whether or not this would have been the principal gate into the castle or, as seems perhaps more plausible, a secondary one designed mostly for convenience, its existence would help explain why the tower's heraldic decoration was concentrated on its W face, rather than the E, where it might otherwise be expected to have attracted more attention.

The southern compartment of the basement would have measured 6.7m N–S by 7.3m E–W, with a rounded bulge on the west corresponding to the internal wall of the Period 4 tower. It has a window in its E wall facing the courtyard; another smaller one high in the eastern part of the S wall was later blocked when the chamber block was built against it. The outside face of the latter was 0.7m wide and 0.4m high, and had a broad chamfer. Possible remains of another similar opening may be observed further east in what is now the N wall of the upper prison (see below). The northern compartment was virtually a mirror image of the southern, except that the window in the N wall lay towards the west and may possibly represent (in its lower parts at least) a feature belonging to the earlier gatehouse. Within the eastern part of the same wall however, a door opened on to a mural stair to the first floor. This was about 1m wide and roofed with sandstone slabs. The stair's treads and the thin wall that separated it from the basement had largely been lost and were restored in 1993 as part of the consolidation programme, making it possible once again to ascend to the upper parts of the tower. Where the stair turned in the corner of the tower it was lit by a deep slit window through the buttress on the tower's NE corner.

The First-Floor Hall

The first floor comprised a large vaulted hall measuring 18m by 17.2/17.6m. Its principal door was located near the N end of the E wall and was approached either by a timber stair from the courtyard or from the first floor of an adjoining building (see below). Although its original jambs and lintel are lost, the door appears to have been about 1.4m wide and 2m high, its slightly splayed passage being roofed with a segmental vault. The service stair from the basement emerged into the hall through the N side of a window recess located between this door and the NE corner of the room; the window itself may have been no more than a slit, but its surrounds are now robbed.

The location of the main door and service stair point to the N end of the hall as having been the 'low' end. The door would most likely have opened into a timber-screened passage, to the north of which would have been the pantry and buttery communicating with the cellar below. In addition to the window on the east, the service area was also lit on the west by another small slit-window and in the N gable wall by a larger splayed window. The head of the latter now consists of a steel beam, above which the wall-face has been rebuilt. It would have had a stone lintel and a segmental rear-arch in its original form. Above this was a smaller window (now blocked) intended to light a timber loft or gallery above the service area. In the E side of this upper window a small door opens into an irregular closet containing a latrine, from which a chute descended to near the base of the external wall. The closet was itself lit from behind the latrine by a slit window.

The S or 'upper' end of the hall was lit by larger windows in the E and W walls. The recesses for these extended down to floor level and they had steps leading up to them, though apparently no seats. The outer arches were pointed, though the voussoirs of the eastern window no longer survive. Both were checked internally for shutters, the rebates for which had a slightly more rounded head than the openings themselves. The jambs of the SW window also bear the trace of a glazing check and the stub of a transom, suggesting (assuming that there was also a mullion) that the lower part of the opening may have been quartered. It is uncertain what would have filled the arch, since whatever was there was not bonded with the voussoirs and has fallen away. It is not improbable, however, that the arch would have been filled with plate or Y tracery.

Both of these windows have pointed rear-arches, which in the case of the W one springs from a pair of figured corbels, sat at its inner edge (Fig 29). The left-hand (S) corbel represents the head, diminutive arms and upper torso of a lady, her hair held in a voluminous cap, which descends to her shoulders on both sides of her face. The right-hand (N) corbel appears to be the corresponding corbel, but represents a knight in armour, wearing a bacinet-type of helmet and with his left shoulder-plate clearly visible. Sadly his face has sheared off, apparently through a natural weakness in the stone rather than an act of vandalism. The profile of what remains gives the impression that he may have had a pointed beard, though it is possible that this is an illusion created by the line of fracture.

Another large window with a splayed segmental rear-arch was set high in the S gable, above the position of the dais. Its dressed surrounds have been robbed and the opening has been rebuilt in rubble, misleadingly with a rounded head. Two other smaller windows were set at the same level mid-way along the hall in the haunches of the vault. These consisted of plain lintelled openings with rounded rear-arches, the lintels being carried forward on corbels to accommodate them into the barrel-vault. Between these windows and the those lighting the high table were a pair of smoke vents, consisting of rounded intersecting vaults similar to those of the high windows' rear-arches, from which vertical slits rose inside the wall apparently to the wall-head (though they are now blocked).

As remarked above, the first-floor hall was floored in timber, except possibly for a strip 5m wide in the centre, which was supported by the vault covering the basement transe. As there were no fireplaces, it may be assumed that heating was provided by braziers, placed perhaps on the stone rather than on the timber parts of the floor; the smoke from these would have dispersed through the windows and vents in the sides of the vault.

A large area of masonry in the eastern part of the S wall has been rebuilt in modern times in order to consolidate the corner of the tower. The trace of a relieving arch in the surviving original masonry however, betrays the former existence of a door which has now been restored at a lower level and with a stone lintel. The original door led into a rectangular lobby covered by a barrel-vault running N–S. To the right (or west) of this, another door (which has also gone) led into a closet, also covered by a vault running N–S. This was lit by a slit-window on the S and had a shouldered-arched aumbry recess on the W. To the left (east) of the lobby a narrow passage led to a turnpike stair to the upper floors. After the addition of the chamber block to the S side of the tower (see below), an opening was apparently forced through the S wall of the lobby to connect with its first floor.

The Second-Floor Hall

The upper hall is more regular in plan than the lower (Figs 29 and 35). It measures internally 18.5m by 17.7m and its floor is 12m above the floor level of the basement. It was covered by a pointed barrel-vault, with transverse and diagonal ribs forming two square bays. A third, narrower bay on the south, corresponding to the service area, was left undecorated. The ribs were carved from yellow sandstone, and were thick, rounded and with a broad keel. They seem to have had little structural purpose, being simply applied to the underside of the vault rather than bonded into it. They sprang from six rounded moulded corbels, from which also sprang four segmental-arched formerets, which defined the base of the barrel-vault on either side of the hall. No such formerets were provided in the screens or service bay; but by some miscalculation the two *tas-de-charges* at the service end were provided with springers for formerets on both sides; this gaffe may not have been very obvious, as the springers facing the service would most probably have been hidden by the screen. Some of the voussoins have masons' marks (Fig 30).

The hall was entered from the turnpike stair in the SE corner of the tower. From this a door, whose jamb and two large holes for hinges survive on the S, opened into a small lobby a little over one metre square. This is still covered by a segmental vault with diagonal ribs applied to its underside. On its S side a slop-basin is recessed into the wall at waist level, its drain simply running out through the wall. The lobby appears to have opened directly into the screens or service area of the hall through a pointed-arch with no second door. Although no trace survives of the timber screen that would have separated the S bay from the rest of the hall, it seems likely that the small entrance lobby would have opened into a larger timber lobby giving access both to the hall and to the service, which would have occupied the rest of this bay towards the W. The service would have been lit by a window in the S wall, of which nothing now survives (a modern opening with a rounded head occupies its presumed location). A barrel-vaulted mural passage or closet led from the right (or western) side of its rear arch. Quite possibly there would also have been a loft or gallery above the service area, accessed perhaps from the turnpike stair or by a separate timber stair.

The upper or northern end of the hall was lit by a broad window recess 2.5m wide in its E wall. All trace of the window itself has now gone. The recess, however, is covered by a segmental arch. A springer surviving *in situ* in the NE corner indicates that the soffit was also decorated with applied diagonal ribs of yellow sandstone, narrow in profile and with broad chamfers. In the N side there is also an aumbry recess.

A pointed-arched opening in the centre of the N wall probably represents 19th-century rebuilding, replacing an original opening of some sort. Through it one or two steps would have led up into a mural passage running E–W. The central part of this was probably once vaulted by a N–S barrel-vault at a higher level than the rest of the passage; its N wall now features a round-headed window, 0.6m wide, whose head at the very least appears to be a modern reconstruction. To the

Fig 35 View of second-floor hall of tower house (Period 6) from S.

right (or E) of this central bay, a short passage covered by three stone lintels runs up to a door, now represented by no more than the right-hand jamb, cut with a plain external chamfer. This opened into a closet containing two latrines, or possibly a slop basin and a latrine: the first drained straight out through the wall, while the second has a chute that descends inside wall almost to ground level. The closet is covered by a segmental vault, running N–S; it has a lamp recess in its S wall and a slit window on the east. The western arm of the passage was covered by pointed barrel-vault and ended in a plain wall, into which is set an aumbry or lamp recess. A gap in the masonry on its N side may possibly represent the location of a window, though the evidence is inconclusive.

There were two other windows in the hall: one on the W side of the N bay, the other on the E side of the central bay. The latter has a segmental rear-arch constructed in sandstone ashlar, though it is now much restored. The original profile of the opening remains uncertain. The other window appears to have been similar, though it is less well preserved.

The hall was originally heated by a single fireplace set in the W wall of the central bay. Most of its sandstone surrounds are now robbed. Enough survives, however, to indicate that its lintel and the trapezoidal hood above it were carried forward on corbels. A second fireplace was inserted in the E wall of the N bay at a later date, perhaps in the 16th century, when the hall was subdivided to form an inner and an outer chamber. The surrounds have mostly been robbed and the lintel or arch replaced, probably in the 19th century, by a segmental arch in split whinstone. Another feature of the 19th-century restoration is a rainwater drain, which runs out through its back wall and was intended to drain the concrete terrace that then paved the hall. As part of the recent consolidation this concrete floor was replaced with flagstone paving incorporating a piped drainage system.

The Upper Floor and Roof

The turnpike stair did not stop at the level of the upper hall, but continued upwards. This has led to speculation that there might have been another floor, containing chambers, or alternatively that such a floor was intended but never built. It is indeed curious that what survives of the original tower-house contains no private chamber, such as one would expect a king to have required in the later 14th century. The floor above the upper hall would already have been some 22m above the basement floor level. To have added another full floor level above that would have made the tower extremely tall relative to its width; and taking account of the outward thrust exerted by the two barrel vaults, this might easily have compromised its stability. None the less, it seems very probable that the terrace roof overlying the upper barrel-vault would have been protected from the rain and snow by a pitched timber roof, shedding water on to the gulleys and spouts on the wall-head. It is perfectly possible that suitably appointed chambers with gabletted windows would have been accommodated within this garret space.

The South Annexe to the Tower-house (Fig 36)

The domestic accommodation available within the tower-house was subsequently greatly augmented by the construction of an annexe containing further chambers against the outside face of its S wall. This structure was 5.5m wide with walls 1.5m thick, providing an additional 35m² of living space on each of its five or more floor levels.

The annexe seems to have been entered from the courtyard to the E by a new stone staircase, 1.8m wide, of which only the masonry base survives (Fig 37). At the top of the stair a door in the now-demolished E wall led into a barrel-vaulted lobby or porter's lodge. From this a forced opening in the S wall of the tower-house would have given access to the bottom of the turnpike stair and to the lower hall. It seems unlikely that the original door at the N end of the lower hall would have gone out of use at this time, as the new access arrangement would have brought guests and others into the hall at the wrong end. It seems more likely that the new stair was intended to improve access to the more private domestic parts of the tower and annexe, including the upper hall, by allowing those wanting to reach them to by-pass the lower hall altogether. Access would nevertheless have been controlled by the porter.

The identification of the room as a porter's lodge is suggested by the existence next to it on the west of a smaller barrel-vaulted room containing a small fireplace and a latrine or slop-basin, with a chute draining diagonally out through the wall. This was evidently a prison or lock-up, intended to house those being held awaiting trial in one or other of the halls. Its floor level is some 0.3m lower than that of the lodge. It was entered through a low doorway, which appears to have been modified at some stage; but since the left-hand jamb is missing the details are not entirely clear. The surviving part of the right-hand jamb has a broad chamfer and indicates, like the check in the wall to the left, that there was originally an outer door, hinged on the right, which opened inwards. The existence of a draw-bar slot in the party wall, however, suggests that there was also an inner door, which opened outwards and could be bolted shut from the outside. It is difficult to tell whether the two doors would have been in use at the same time.

The pit prison was cleared of building debris in 1986. It measured 3.3 by 1.85m, and its floor, 2.5m below the trap-door, consisted of trodden clay-rich till overlying bedrock, levelled up in part with dumps of mortar-bonded stones. The walls were unfaced and were built using generally smaller stones than those in the S wall of the tower-house, which they abutted. The vaulting runs E–W, with the N side of the vault supported on masonry built against the S face of the tower-house.

Below the porter's lodge and next to the pit prison, though separate from it, was another room covered by a semi-vault leaning against the wall of the tower. This was entered from the courtyard though a door and a diagonal passage set within the base of the external staircase. A rough rounded opening in the E wall provided minimal lighting, but seems unlikely to be an original feature. Indeed two of the stones around it appear to have been crudely worked *in situ*. Its sill is formed from the reused base of a fish-tail arrow-slit, quite possibly derived from a dismantled part of the 13th-century castle. This basement was excavated over two seasons from 1986. Some 4m of debris had accumulated outside it and similar material filled the interior; most of this appeared to be discarded rubble from the destroyed parts of the S annexe. It seems indeed that this room and the pit prison had been deliberately infilled with rubble at some time, possibly in order to help stabilise the base of the tower or simply as part of a general exercise in land-scaping.

It may be assumed that the upper floors of the annexe would have been reached up the turnpike stair in the SE angle of the tower-house, though no trace of doorways now survives. Indeed at second-floor level not even the floor survives in the part next to the stair. This floor, carried on barrel-vaults, would have been at roughly the same level as the loft or gallery at the N end of the lower hall; however, since there was no corresponding entresol floor at the S end, it may be assumed that the S window would have been blocked in this phase. The second floor appears to have comprised a single room, 3.7/3.9 by 8.9m, though the possibility of there having been a timber subdivision cannot be discounted. It was lit by two splayed windows on the S; the W wall contained no openings, while the E wall, no longer stands, contained a door leading out to the barmkin wall-head.

The third floor was roughly level with the upper hall inside the tower-house. The floor itself was of timber. The evidence for this is provided by the survival of six corbels on the S wall and three on the north, which evidently once supported the wall-plates on which the ends of the joists rested. It had a splayed window in the W wall and another in the middle of the south, both somewhat larger than those of the floor below. The E wall is lost. The positioning of the windows makes it unlikely that the room was subdivided. It may possibly have communicated with the service end of the hall through a former window in the latter's S wall; alternatively the window may simply have been blocked in this period.

Fig 36 View of the S annexe to the tower house (Period 6) from E.

Fig 37 View of foundations for stair to ground floor of the S annexe (Period 6) from E.

The existence of a fourth floor 4m above the third is attested by the survival of a further four corbels set into the S wall of the tower-house. The roof, perhaps a simple pentice, was probably immediately above this.

Structure 21 (Figs 18 and 38)

The remains of a rectangular, barrel-vaulted stone building lying E of the tower-house and aligned E–W were investigated over two short seasons of excavation in 1991 and 1993. Although the W gable wall [1027] of this building was still largely intact, the other walls were not visible before excavation began. Unfortunately it was not possible to carry the excavation right up to wall [1027] for fear of undermining the scaffolding associated with the masonry consolidation of the tower then in progress. However, it was extended far enough to the east to attempt to determine the northward extent of a later wall [1011], separating the inner and outer courts of the barmkin in Period 6.

The outline of the building was revealed, along with accumulated debris from its own demolition and from later clearance work. The infill over both rooms had also been truncated by two modern features: an electric cable trench and a series of wooden fence posts running roughly N–S.

The building was constructed in lime-mortared rubble. It was rectangular and measured 5.4m N–S by 6.76m E–W internally, and 7.6m N–S by 8.85m E–W externally. The W gable still stands 3.5m high and is about 1m thick. On its E face there is still just discernible the outline of a low rounded barrel-vault that would appear to have covered the ground floor. This wall has been extensively repaired even to the extent of having its base supported with a pad of grey cement mortar of the type used for consolidating the tower-house in the early 20th century. The N and S walls had been extensively robbed of their facing stones, leaving only a core 0.6–0.9m thick, whereas the E wall survived in better condition. The latter was similar in build and width to the W gable, and was significantly narrower than the later enclosure wall [021/1011] which abutted it. It is possible that the building had been constructed over the remains of an earlier smaller structure, as the S wall thickened externally about halfway along its length and the N wall also widened slightly at a similar point.

Given the steep drop in level between the base of the wall at its NW corner and the height of bedrock encountered towards its SE interior corner, there may have been a need for a raised floor at ground level. There was no evidence of a doorway in any of the walls, although there was a slight indication of what may possibly have been an entrance in the S wall towards the SW corner.

The building's roof, or first floor if it had one, would have been roughly level with the first-floor doorway into the tower-house. Indeed, the structure appears to have been built directly against – or to have incorporated – an enclosure wall that ran E from the NE corner of the tower. It is uncertain whether it acted as some kind of fore-building to the tower, or whether the stair to the first-floor door into the tower was of timber and stood in the space between the tower and the building's W gable. The latter is perhaps unlikely, as such a stair would have had to have been very steep to have fitted into the available space, and it would have blocked what appears to have been the principal way into the inner barmkin (see below).

Fig 38 View from NE of the E façade of the tower house (Period 6) with Structure 21 (Period 4?) in foreground.

The demolished remains of the building were subsequently levelled up with
a series of tipped deposits, perhaps to facilitate access during the initial phases
of clearance of the tower in modern times. These comprised rubble and mortar
scatters, deepening to the west and north, suggesting that they had been tipped
from the south and east. A division in the tips along the line of wall [1019/1020]
was noted and interpreted as indicating that the wall had been standing during
the time when some of the infilling was being done. During the excavations this
facilitated the separation of the different periods of backfilling and demolition
within the building from one another.

The Barmkin Wall (Fig 39)

The construction of the S annexe to the tower-house was soon followed by the
construction of a new enclosure wall or barmkin replacing that of the destroyed
13th-century castle. It enclosed the upper two terraces of the castle rock and
extended around the higher parts of the hill (Fig 8). The circuit was entered by a
gate on the E, the original dimensions of which are not clear as it was subsequently
remodelled to a narrow doorway only 2m wide. The S wall was set out in line with
the S wall of the annexe and ran in a straight line for 13.4m before turning slightly
northwards and continuing for 7.3m up to the SE angle. From here the wall ran
10m northward up to the E gate, then a further 5m to the NW corner. The N wall
ran in a straight line to an uncertain point somewhere close to the north-western
corner of the tower-house. Although in order to complete the enclosure the
barmkin wall is likely to have ended by abutting the tower-house, there is nothing
to indicate where it did so. Possibly it abutted the tower at or near its NE corner,
thereby allowing the tower's latrines to empty themselves outside the walls. It is
alternatively possible that the wall continued westward to enclose the terrace on
the west side of the tower, thus allowing those entering the barmkin from the east
to proceed around the N side of the tower and enter it through its now-blocked W
door.

The barmkin wall would once have stood to an impressive height, no doubt
with a parapeted wall-walk around its entire circuit. This structure, however, has
suffered more than any other element of the Period 6 castle as a result of stone
robbing. This is particularly so on its S and E sides, where it has been reduced to
about 2m in height from an original 8m. At the point where it abutted the SE corner
of the annexe, however, traces may still be seen of the parapet and the S reveal of
a door opening on to the wall-walk from the second-floor chamber (Fig 30).

On the east side of the tower the barmkin was subdivided by a crosswall
[021/1011] (Figs 6, 18) to form an inner courtyard immediately next to the tower.
This crosswall appears to be of one build with the barmkin wall itself. It ran north
from the S barmkin wall to abut the SE corner of Structure 21, which appears to
have been incorporated into it. The gap, some 2.5m wide between the NW corner
of the same building and the NE corner of the tower, was also closed by a wall,
whose abutment is still clearly visible in elevation on the tower's external wall. It
was 1.5m thick and stood 7m high. Above it there survives the outline of a parapet
2m high, which projected forward from the outer face of the wall by as much as a
metre. Such a projection seems excessive for a corbelled machicolation, though it

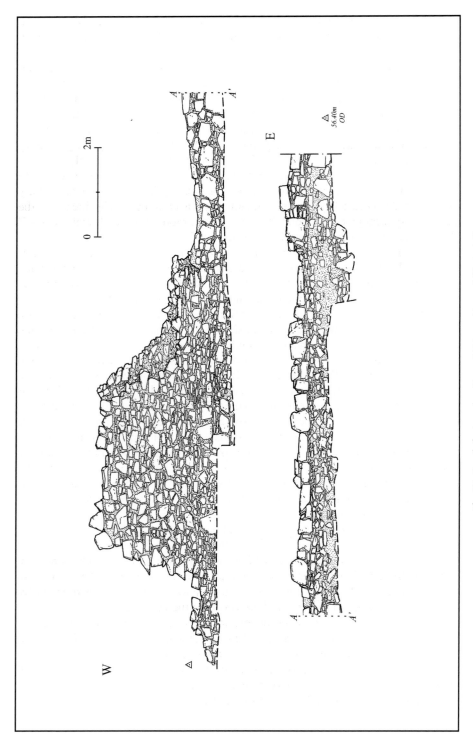

Fig 39 South-facing elevation of N barmkin wall (Period 6).

could perhaps have been part of a bartizan or a wall-head latrine set in the external angle between the tower and the wall. It may be noted that the tower-house's own latrines are also located in this area.

If the space between the tower and Structure 21 had been closed by a solid wall, however, the question arises of how access was gained to the inner court from the outer barmkin. One possibility is that the main route into the inner barmkin lay through the tower's W door and the transe in its basement; however, this would have been exceptionally circuitous and the door in the tower's E wall is inconveniently narrow. Another possibility is that there was originally an entry into the inner court in the crosswall [021/1011] itself; this seems unlikely since the wall is relatively well preserved and no trace of any opening can be seen today. In any case, a series of other structures was later built against its E side, apparently ruling out the possibility of there having been a door in it. The idea that the entrance lay through Structure 21 itself is perhaps more feasible, though the E–W alignment and low height of its barrel-vault would have made any such entrance somewhat inconvenient. This leaves the gap between Structure 21 and the tower as the likeliest position for the entrance into the inner court. Unfortunately this area was not excavated, since at the time of the excavations it was partly blocked by large sections of collapsed masonry and obscured by scaffolding.

Whether or not the gate into the barmkin lay between the tower and Structure 21, however, also affects our understanding of how access was gained into the tower. From the inner courtyard, normal access to the tower would have been either by means of the stone forestair and guard room in the S annexe or through the first-floor door to the lower hall. If there had been a solid wall between the tower and Structure 21, it is just possible that there could have been a timber stair leading to this door in the area of dead space thus created, though as already remarked the stair would have been very steep. If the main gate to the inner barmkin had been located there, however, there could clearly have been no stair in that position. In that case, it is possible that the tower's first-floor door was reached either from the first floor of Structure 21, which might thus be interpreted as part of a gatehouse range, or by some form of external timber gallery built over the entrance passage into the barmkin and reached by a stair located further E.

Structure 22 (Fig 18)

Structure 21 was subsequently extended 3.3m to the east by the addition of an annexe (Structure 22), tacked on to its E side. The relationship of Structure 21 to the crosswall [021/1011] is uncertain; however, a row of buildings (Structures 18, 20, 19) was later built against it and the E side of the crosswall.

Other than the presence of a probable doorway in the S wall, later modified to allow access to Structure 18, there is little indication of the original function of Structure 22. It is uncertain, for example, whether there was internal communication between it and Structure 21, whether its purpose was to extend whatever stood at first-floor level above Structure 21, or whether it was simply an ancillary building like those later added to the south of it.

Structure 18 (Fig 18)

Excavation immediately south of Structure 22 revealed the remains of a stone-built but relatively crudely constructed chamber. The building was defined by two earth-bonded walls to the south and east, which abutted [1011] and the S walls of Structure 22 and formed its W and N walls respectively.

The resulting chamber measured 5.5m N–S by 3.4m E–W internally and appears to have been a small service building rather than a domestic structure. There was a doorway in its E wall giving access on to a crudely flagged floor surface or threshold. In the NW corner was a simple stone platform measuring *c*. 1.0m by 1.2m standing about 0.3m above the general floor area, while in the S wall was a possible 'firebreak' associated with a hearth. These features suggest that the building may perhaps have been used as a smiddy.

It is likely that in addition to its E doorway, Structure 18 provided access to Structure 22 in some way, as the doorway of the latter seems to have been crudely widened and possibly lowered for ease of access from Structure 18.

Structure 20 (Fig 18)

Immediately south of Structure 18 was Structure 20. This was the same width as Structure 18, measuring 7m by 4m internally. The E wall was very poorly preserved and may in any case not have been completed. The evidence of a distinctive step-like construction, built against the E face of crosswall [021/1011] and running the full length of the building, suggests that it may have served as a stable or byre. This is also suggested by its distinctively superior cobbled floor and by its location next to the workshop or smiddy in Structure 18.

Structure 19 (Fig 18)

This range of buildings comprised three elements built beside the remains of Period 3 Structure 16b. It ran E–W over three 'rooms' for a distance of 14.66m with a minimum width of 4.5m, generally comparable to Structures 18 and 20. However, it was defined on its S side not by the barmkin wall, but by its own separate S wall [064]. This suggested that it was distinct from the lean-to structures running N–S (18 and 20). Structure 19 may therefore be interpreted as a separate, largely free-standing building.

The W gable of Structure 19 was formed by the crosswall [021/1011] and its westernmost chamber measured 4m by 5m. It had a simple hearth lying 1.2m E of [021/1011] along the central E–W line of the building. The remains of a central and E chamber were extremely badly preserved, but each may also have had a hearth site.

The fabric of this building and its fellow outer courtyard structures was of clay- or soil-bonded stonework, the poor quality of which suggested that they never stood to any great height. The compartmental form and the relatively narrow width could facilitate sturdy roof construction, though whether or not they were slated was not clear.

The subsequent conversion of the eastern chamber of Structure 19 in Phase 7 (see below) to form Structure 23 massively disrupted the N line of Structure 19 and the evidence for its N wall was not clear. Areas of metalling over the remains of the Structure 16b group of features indicate that it would have been 5m wide. It must certainly have been entered from the north, most likely with a separate door to each compartment, as the gap between barmkin wall and Structure 19 was only about one metre wide.

The purpose of the building remains uncertain, though the existence of hearths suggests that it may perhaps have provided accommodation for servants and stable-hands.

The Cistern (Fig 40)

The provision of a new water supply in the form of a massive open cistern represented another element in the upgrading of the castle. This structure was created by re-lining in stone a deep irregular pit, cut into bedrock in the northern half of the barmkin enclosure. The pit may simply have been one of several quarries for stone used in the construction of the S annexe or tower-house; but, by the digging of such a hole, the presence of water may well have suggested a second and more long-term use for it. By this time the well in the 13th-century E gate-house would have been out of use; and it would in any case have now been located outside the new barmkin wall.

The cistern consisted of a rectangular enclosure, faced on three sides with rough masonry, partly mortar bonded, the other face being simply the vertical face of the bedrock itself. It measured 2.7 by 3m internally and water was found at a depth of 1.2m below the surviving wall-head. It is possible that it was roofed, if only to keep the water clear and provide a working platform over it; but no evidence of any such covering survived. It is uncertain if this was the main water source for the Period 6 or even if the water in it was intended for human consumption; its capacity, however, suggests that it could have supplied a large community. Finds from the backfill of the original rock-cut pit, behind the stone lining, suggest a late 14th-century/early 15th-century date for the cistern's construction. This context contained a good assemblage of pottery, including several almost complete vessels.

Within the broad dating framework of the medieval castle, which is based to some extent on pottery types and fabrics, the construction of the cistern coincides with the abandonment of the well in the E gatehouse. This we know to have been retained into Period 5 but to have been abandoned by the first half of the 15th century. The backfill of the well contained pottery of similar date to that encountered in the general infill of the ruined E gatehouse as well as other artefacts. These included three bone-handled implements of very superior craftsmanship which may well have been deposited in some form of bag. In addition, in and around the demolished and levelled gatehouse towers were found several examples of incised slates, ranging from very simple scratched designs, to one example which depicted, albeit crudely, two figures, carrying double-handed swords with angled quillons, of a type generally regarded as 15th century in date (Figs 48 and 49).

Fig 40 View from S of open cistern (Period 6) to the left with possible stone quarry to the right.

PERIOD 7: *c.* 1449/50–*c.* 1588/9 (Fig 18)

The reduction in the scale of the household resident at Dundonald during Period 7 is demonstrated by the decline of Structure 19 and its replacement with Structure 23. This was built over the remains of the E chamber of Structure 19 and ran further northwards and southwards. Walls from Structure 19 were extended to the S by the addition of two short sections only 1.5m long, in order to abut the inside face of the barmkin enclosure. To the N they were lengthened creating a building 9m by 5.5m with a doorway in its E wall. Structure 23 may also have featured a small building or yard to the W, also recycling Structure 19 masonry (064). The former was of very poor construction and showed no sign of domestic usage other than perhaps later squatter occupation. It may therefore have been some sort of storehouse or general purpose bothy for the later occupants of the castle in their increasingly straitened circumstances.

4 The Artefact Assemblage

CERAMICS

by David Caldwell and Ewan Campbell

Although the ceramics from these excavations derive from all phases of occupation, the collection is not large. There are no complete, or near complete vessels, and many of the sherds are very small. Nevertheless, this is an invaluable corpus from an important site in a part of Scotland where the medieval pottery industry has been little studied or understood. The complex nature of the stratification and phasing at the castle, with many sherds undoubtedly being redeposited in later contexts, further limits the scope for close dating of any of the ceramics.

The fabric analysis is based solely upon visual examination using a binocular microscope at ×20 where appropriate. The colour descriptions and classifications are taken from the Munsell Color Charts. All the material is assumed to be Scottish, most probably of local origin, with the exception of the Imported Early Historic pottery.

Prehistoric Pottery (Fig 41)

by David Caldwell

Approximately 170 sherds of very coarse plain prehistoric pottery were recovered. Apart from one small rim sherd (no. 1) distinguished by its more compact fabric, the pottery could derive from a single coarse vessel. This exceptional rim sherd is too small to permit accurate assessment of the original form and size of the vessel, but in the light of associated archaeological evidence it probably derives from a simple bucket-shaped pot, perhaps with a slightly closed rim. While stressing the need for caution, parallels for such pottery might be sought among the pottery from, broadly speaking, Late Bronze Age/Early Iron Age sites. Analogous material has been found in the region at Carwinning Hill, Dalry (Cowie forthcoming).

As already remarked, the remaining pottery (nos 2–5) could conceivably derive from a single very coarse vessel. Only a single small rim sherd is present (no. 2a) and this is again too small to permit accurate assessment of the original form and size of the vessel. However, it probably derives from a thick-walled bucket-shaped pot, possibly with a slightly closed rim, and probably a proportionately broad base. The fabric is the most distinctive feature: it is extremely coarse and very thick (up to 20mm), with large stone inclusions but also traces of profuse organic inclusions in the form of voids or channels in the thickness of the wall. In one case, traces of applied material appear to be present in the clay. Traces of grooves are present on the exterior surface of several sherds; they do not appear

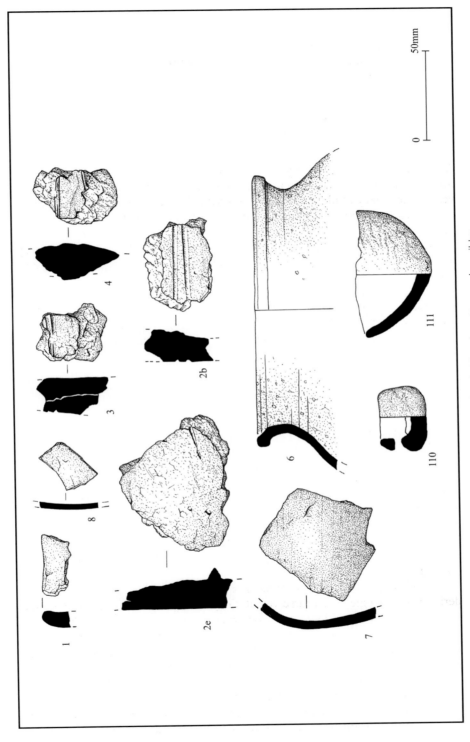

Fig 41 Prehistoric and Early Historic pottery and crucibles.

to be a decorative feature, but perhaps rather the remains of organic binding. Much of the inner surface is wanting as a result of lamination, resulting in exposure of the heavily gritted core. The external surfaces show pronounced thumbing/fingertipping of the clay with many signs of where the clay has been worked during building. The pot has been constructed using simple angled building joints, but the general impression is of a pot that has been built up almost like daub, perhaps reflecting a particular functional requirement.

This general combination of features invites comparison with the very coarse pottery recovered from several Scottish vitrified forts such as Finavon, Dunagoil and also similar material from Kilellan Farm, Islay (Ritchie and Welfare 1983, 323–31).

In summary, parts of a minimum of two vessels were found. With due caution in view of their fragmentary condition, a Late Bronze Age/Early Iron Age date would be reasonable (in broad terms 1st millennium BC).

1   Rim sherd; simple rim, harder fabric than the rest of the prehistoric pottery; 14 × 34mm; 10mm thick at break [102].

2(a) Rim sherd; simple rim, too small to permit assessment of form and size; 17 × 17mm [125/138]. Not illustrated.

2(b) Body fragment, with traces of two converging grooves on external surface; 53 × 57mm.

2(c) Body fragment, with traces of a groove on external surface; 48 × 39mm. Not illustrated.

2(d) Four fragments of basal angle all from the same vessel, but too small to permit assessment of form and size; largest c. 48 × 48mm. Not illustrated.

2(e) Approximately 160 body fragments and crumbs; largest 77 × 63mm.

3   Body sherd, with traces of grooves on external surface; 38 × 35mm; 20mm thick; broken along building joint [099].

4   Body sherd, with traces of grooves on external surface; 45 × 35mm; 18.5mm thick; broken along building join. SF 34 [121].

5   Three body fragments, largest 40 × 30mm [138/82]. Not illustrated.

Early Historic Imported Pottery (Fig 41)

by Ewan Campbell

The Early Historic pottery consists of three sherds of Thomas's Class E ware (Thomas 1959); a rim and two bodysherds from one or possibly two vessels. The rim and upper bodysherd probably join, and are certainly from the same vessel. The lower bodysherd is suffiently similar in fabric and thickness to be of the same vessel, but this is not certain. The form of the vessel is a standard E1 jar or *olla*. There are some 230 or so known vessels of E ware from around 75 sites in western Britain and Ireland, with the E1 jar being by far the commonest form. The minor characteristics of the rim form in E ware are variable, depending on the idiosyncrasies of individual potters, and this example is not identical to any other vessel.

6/7 Rim and shoulder sherds of E1 jar. Rim everted, squared, with slight internal lid-seat, well-finished, with rillmarks. Exterior with fingerprint from lifting the pot off the wheel. Colour variable, beige to black, exterior with sooting. Fabric coarse gritty with characteristic pimply surface and laminated texture, inclusions only abundant ill-sorted angular/sub-angular quartz grains up to 2mm. Sherds fresh, unabraded. Rim diameter 15cm, 80°. Maximum body diameter 18cm. Maximum sherd size 9cm and 6cm. Rim: DC87/SF46/TR:D 001(W); body sherd DC87/SF42.

8   Lower bodysherd, possibly from the same vessel. Fabric as above. Interior has pale purple stain. Unabraded. Thickness 7–8mm. Maximum sherd size 4cm. DC86/058.

Discussion

E ware can now be dated to the later 6th and 7th centuries, with a floruit in the early 7th century (for this and the following discussion see Campbell 1996; forthcoming). The exact provenance is not known, though almost certainly lies in western coastal France between the Loire and Gironde estuaries. The pottery was brought to western Britain and Ireland as part of a trading system which targeted important secular sites, mainly in coastal locations. These sites share a suite of characteristics: they are fortified; they show evidence of craft specialisation and fine metalworking of brooches; they have precious metals; and they often have documented royal status or associations. These centres of importation seem to have acted as redistributive centres to subsidiary aristocratic sites in their hinterland. The secondary sites usually produce only a few imported vessels, and do not have the listed characteristics of the primary import centres. The pottery was often accompanied by imported glass with distinctive white trailing, but the quantities involved suggest that neither the pottery nor the glass was likely to have been the major traded item. Bulk perishable goods such as wine and salt are exports of western France at the period and these may have been the major cargoes.

The E ware itself was probably not imported as pottery, but as containers for luxury goods. Traces of purple or red dyestuff on some vessel interiors have been analysed and show the presence of Dyer's madder (*Rubia tincorum*), a plant not native to NW Europe, but which documentary evidence shows was grown on royal estates in Carolingian France and exported from markets there. The stains on the Dundonald sherd are a vivid illustration of this process. Other sites which have produced purple dye on E ware are: Buiston crannog, Ayrshire; Dunadd fort and Loch Glashan crannog, Argyll; and Teeshan crannog, Co. Antrim. Other items such as exotic nuts, spices and sweetmeats could have been traded in the E ware jars, and indeed seeds of the exotic culinary plants coriander and dill have been recently found at Buiston crannog (Crone 2000, 152–3) and Whithorn (Hill 1997, 124), at both sites in association with E ware. Access to these imported luxury goods would have been used by local rulers to help reinforce and sustain their status, with the distribution of small amounts to nobles under their control. The distribution of E ware around these central sites would give an indication in the archaeological record of the extent of these sites' influence.

Continental imports have been found at three other sites within the ancient British kingdoms of the Central valley: E ware at Dumbarton Rock (Alcock and Alcock 1990, Fig 13), and within Ayrshire at Buiston crannog (Munro 1882, fig 250; Crone 2000, 158–51, fig 123) and Lochlee crannog (Munro 1882, 138); while continental glass is known from Castle Hill, Dalry (Alcock and Alcock 1990, illus 15) as well as at the three sites with E ware. None of these sites has produced large quantities of imports comparable with the most productive sites in Scotland: Dunadd, Argyll (Lane and Campbell 2000, 98–103), and Whithorn Priory (Campbell 1997). Dundonald is interesting in that its physical and historical characteristics correspond to other major royal sites such as Dunadd and Dumbarton Rock being situated on a low-lying but prominent craggy hill, not far from the coast, and near a river estuary.

Without further indication of the scale of the imports on the site, it is impossible to decide whether Dundonald would have been a major import centre or a secondary redistributive site, though in either case it would have been of significantly high status in the 7th century AD. If it was a central site, it could be argued that it was the centre of redistribution for other sites in Ayrshire such as Buiston crannog. The presence of purple dye on the Dundonald sherd is matched by one example from Buiston, suggesting a possible link between the sites. As Dundonald is not situated on the coast, an actual landing site for foreign merchants has to be postulated in the area, perhaps at Troon or Irvine, or, by analogy with other Irish and Scottish sites, on one of the small offshore islands such as Lady Isle.

Crucibles (Fig 41)

These vessels were used for the working of non-ferous metals. In form 110 is similar to the Type E crucibles while 111 may be Type C from Dunadd both of which date to the Early Historic period (Lane and Campbell 2000, 141–2).

110   A small, roughly cylindrical bowl-shaped ceramic crucible, pierced by a small hole in one side. SF 32 [082].
111   A triangular-mouthed ceramic crucible. SF 144 [748].

Medieval Pottery

by David Caldwell

Light Gritty Wares (Fig 42)
This is a relatively large and amorphous group of sherds, varying considerably in colour. The 'light' in the name refers to the generally lighter range of these colours, for example white, grey, yellow and pink. There are 422 sherds with a total weight of about 2.6kg. They appear to have come from well-made, thin-walled vessels, probably mostly jugs, some decorated with combing, applied strips and pads of decoration. The fabric varies from soft to hard and often has a rough pimply feel due to the poorly sorted rock fragments, including quartz and haematite, some up to 1.5mm across. Inclusions vary considerably in quantity but are normally less than 5%. Light Gritty wares might be expected to range in date from the 12th to as late as the early 15th century. The variety in this group may reflect a lack of consistency in clay preparation and firing rather than several different production centres. Nevertheless, three sub-groups have been distinguished from the mass, and are listed below as 4(i) to (iii).

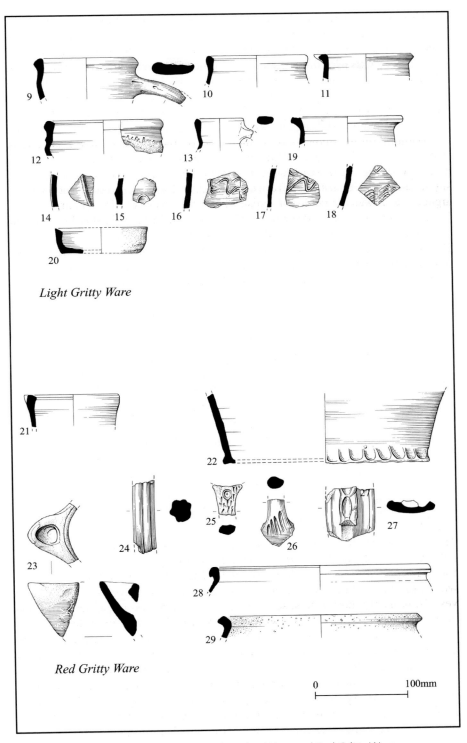

Fig 42 Medieval Pottery: Light Gritty Ware and Red Gritty Ware.

(i) A hard, white to very pale brown (10YR 8/3) fabric with a tendency to feel rough to the touch. It has a fine fracture containing 5% or less sub-rounded pieces of rock, some over 1mm across, including a few pieces of quartz.

(ii) A base sherd with thumbed decoration in a hard, smooth, fine, pink (7.5YR 7/4) fabric with a light grey core. It contains 10% inclusions: angular pieces of rock up to 1mm across, small rounded pieces of iron, and a high percentage of mica.

(iii) A hard, smooth fabric, all the sherds of which have a bright green, streaky glaze, the colour of which has apparently been enhanced by the addition of copper. There are three colour zones within the thickness of the body: white under the glaze, grey core and reddish yellow (7.5YR 7/6) interior surface. The sherds have a fine fracture with 10% small (0.2mm or less) grains of quartz, haematite and rounded voids. Possibly English.

9	Jug rim with strap handle, glazed on the exterior.
10	Jug rim, glazed on the exterior. [936].
11	Jug rim. [757].
12	Jug rim with incised decoration, glazed on exterior. [757].
13	Rim of small jug with rod handle. [118].
14	Body sherd, glazed, decorated with applied strip of clay. [514].
15	Body sherd, glazed on the exterior and with incised decoration. [712].
16–18	Body sherds, glazed on the exterior and with combed decoration. [707].
19	Cooking-pot rim. [939].
20	Sherd, part of the side of a shallow dish, perhaps a dripping pan. [712].

Red Gritty Wares (Fig 42)

This fabric is light red (2.5YR 6/6) or pink (5YR 7/4) in colour, often with a reduced dark grey core and a grey layer beneath a glazed surface. It is hard, smooth or slightly rough to the touch, and contains less than 5% inclusions: poorly sorted quartz, up to 0.5mm across, mica, and small pieces of iron. There are also a few linear voids. The sherds are relatively thin walled and tend to have a pimply surface. The glaze is mostly olive but can also be yellow. A few sherds have a white slip.

There are 287 sherds with a total weight of 2kg, and they evidently consist of jugs and so-called cooking pots, though few were observed to have any sooting on them. The glaze is in all cases on the exterior surface. Jugs had broad bases, thumbed around their edge, and strap or rod handles. Rims were thickened, either rounded, flat on top or triangular in profile. Spouts were simply pulled, but there is one fat bridge spout from a vessel with a slipped interior. Cooking pots had either rectangular or rounded rims. A date range mostly in the 13th and 14th centuries is offered.

21	Jug rim [511].
22	Thumbed base [500].
23	Bridge-spout with decorative thumbing [751].
24	Rod handle, decoratively grooved [759].
25	Handle with stab marks and a ring-and-dot motif [056].
26	Handle bottom, glazed, formed as a hand [759].

27   Strap-handle, glazed, with applied thumbed strip [706].
28   Cooking-pot rim [757].
29   Cooking-pot rim [103].

Reduced Gritty Wares (Fig 43)

(i) This is a hard, highly fired, reduced fabric, finely potted with relatively thin body. The sherds may derive solely from jugs. One base sherd is decorated with thumbing. All are glazed on the exterior, two with incised decoration and two with applied dark brown vertical strips. The glaze is olive coloured, in some cases with a speckled appearance. There are 83 sherds in all with a combined weight of about 1kg. The body sherds vary from very dark grey to grey, with, in some sherds, a clearly defined light grey zone beneath the glaze. The glaze is olive and unglazed exterior surfaces sometimes have a yellowish brown skin. This fabric feels rough, breaks with an irregular edge, and contains 10% or less grains of sub-angular quartz 0.5mm or smaller in size, mica, and linear voids. It may belong to the late 13th and 14th century.

(ii) The bulk of this medieval gritty fabric is a hard reduced fabric, the sherds tending to be smoother and thicker than group (i). They contain 5% or less grains of sub-rounded quartz, less than 0.5mm across, mica, linear voids and specks of iron. The body is grey or dark grey, sometimes with a clearly defined light grey layer beneath olive lead glaze, or a thicker reddish yellow zone with a red skin when not covered by glaze. There are 273 sherds with a total weight of about 9kg. All the sherds could derive from jugs. Rims are thickened and rounded. One shoulder sherd has incised zigzag lines; another body sherd has a thumbed strip. The lower portions of some vessels have been trimmed with a knife prior to firing. The bulk of this pottery may date to the late 14th and 15th century.

(iii) Three sherds, probably all from the one vessel, of grey ware, with a dark grey core and a thin white zone under the glazed exterior. One has an applied strip of white clay on its exterior. The fabric is soft, fine and rough to the feel. It contains 10% sub-angular pieces of quartz, 0.2mm across.

30   Jug rim [004].
31   Base with thumbed decoration [500].
32   Body sherd with incised decoration [103].
33   Body sherd with incised decoration [901].
34   Body sherd with applied, notched strips.
35   Jug rim with strap handle [744].
36   Body sherd with applied thumbed strip [004].

Medieval Smooth Wares (Fig 43)

(i) This fabric comprises a white firing clay and varies from soft and crumbly to hard with a fine texture. Surfaces have a soapy feel and vary from white to pink (7.5YR 8–8/4) with a light grey or grey core, depending on the extent of the reduction in the firing process. Exterior surfaces where the glaze has not taken have a reddish brown (2.5YR 8/4) surface skin. The glaze is olive yellow or yellowish brown in colour. There are fewer than 5% inclusions but these include small rounded grains of quartz, less than 0.2mm in diameter, small specks of iron

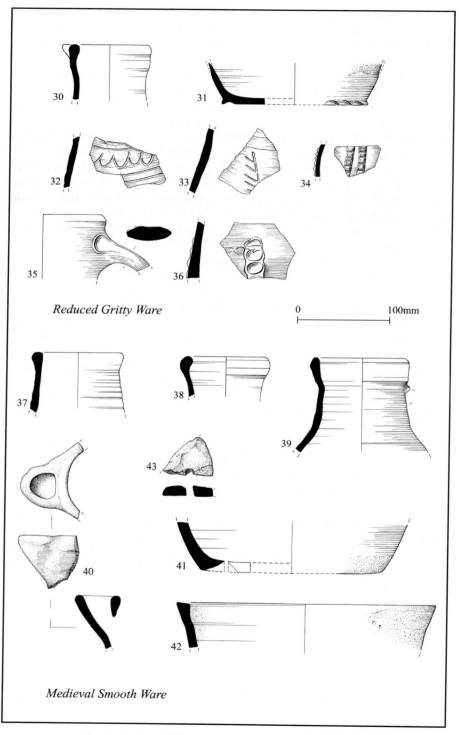

Reduced Gritty Ware

0   100mm

Medieval Smooth Ware

Fig 43 Reduced Gritty Ware and Medieval Smooth Ware.

and occasional rock fragments. There are 213 sherds with a combined weight of about 3.5kg, and these could all be from jugs with relatively thick walls, simple rounded rims and flat bases. They may mostly belong to the 14th and 15th centuries.

(ii) Sherds in this group may be characterised as red. They tend to have reddish yellow (7.5YR 8/6) exterior surfaces and light brownish grey interior surfaces, sometimes with a darker, grey reduced zone in between. The exterior surfaces have olive lead glaze, and where this has not taken, there is a weak red skin. Otherwise the fabric is similar to group (i). There are 118 sherds with a total weight of about 3.3kg. Most of the vessels represented would seem to be jugs with rounded rims and flat bases. There is one fat bridge-spout. One sherd has a series of slashes around its edge, another an applied and thumbed decoration. Some sherds, including the rim of a large bowl and pieces possibly from a dripping dish, have a very pale brown surface and no glaze. One base sherd has been pierced with a hole after firing, possibly to turn it into a watering-jug. Another pierced sherd may be part of a weight or spindle whorl. A late 14th- or 15th-century date may be suggested for this group.

(iii) This is a hard, smooth fabric with bright, reddish yellow (5YR 6/8) or white under-glaze surfaces and, normally, a very dark grey core, forming clear colour zones. Otherwise it appears similar to groups (i) and (ii). There are no rim sherds but the vessels represented – at least three – are likely to have been jugs, covered with lead glaze with an olive hue. There are 20 sherds. This fabric may date to the 15th and early 16th century.

(iv) A soft fabric with almost no inclusions apart from iron. It is represented by one base sherd of a turned vessel, formed into a square with rounded corners, reddish yellow (7.5YR 7/6) in colour with a grey core. Stenhouse-type ware, 15th to 16th century, from the Forth Valley.

(v) Two sherds of a grey, hard fabric with reddish yellow (7.5YR 7/8) surface where not covered in glaze. The fabric has a smooth fracture and contains almost no inclusions apart from the occasional small piece of quartz and speck of iron. Throsk-type ware, 17th century, from the Forth Valley.

(vi) One sherd of a smooth pinkish white (7.5YR 8/2) hard fabric with a fine fracture containing a few specks of iron.

(vii) One sherd of a grooved, glazed, strap handle in a pink (7.5YR 7/4), soft, fine fabric with sparse quartz, haematite, limestone, mica and voids. French.

(viii) Three joining sherds from a ridged rod handle in a pink (5YR 8/4) fabric covered with a greenish brown glaze. It is soft and fine and contains sparse quartz grains. Dutch.

37   Jug rim and neck [1200].
38   Jug rim [503].
39   Jug rim and shoulders [177].
40   Bridge-spout [727].
41   Base sherd with secondary piercing [707].
42   Rim, possibly from a large bowl [051].
43   Sherd with piercing [707].

Discussion of the Medieval Pottery

Looking at the corpus of medieval pottery as a whole, the lack of identified imports from England or further afield may seem surprising, but this bears out the conclusions on the assemblages of pottery from recent excavations: almost all the North European pottery from Scotland, as listed by Thoms (1983), is found in the east of the country. It is possible, therefore, that the Dundonald Castle assemblage contains pottery brought in from other regions of Scotland. This would seem to be the case with the group 7(iv) base sherd. Its fabric bears a distinct resemblance to ceramics from the Forth Valley, for example from the kiln site at Stenhouse, near Falkirk, and the vessel form can be paralleled by another base sherd from Linlithgow Palace.

On balance it appears reasonable to suppose that the bulk of the pottery from Dundonald Castle is of local manufacture. Our understanding of the different fabrics represented in the assemblage is too incomplete to indicate whether several, or perhaps even just one, production centre was involved in the supply of wares.

The Light Gritty Ware sherds are superficially similar to white gritty pottery from elsewhere in Scotland, including material from excavations in Ayr. This pottery has often been described as an east coast tradition, with an identified production centre at Colstoun in East Lothian (Brooks 1980), and others predicted for Fife and in the vicinity of the important medieval burgh of Roxburgh in the Borders. A superficial comparison of thin-section slides (in the National Museums of Scotland) of pottery from Ayr with pottery from Kelso Abbey, the Colstoun kiln site and places in Fife, does not suggest a need to look to the east of the country as a source of most of the Ayrshire pottery. A major study of the White Gritty Ware tradition involving formal and chemical analyses (Jones *et al.* in press) will provide a more up-to-date assessment of these wares.

Two of the most important criteria used in arranging the Dundonald Castle assemblage in fabric groups were colour, and range and density of inclusions. The assumption is often made by students of pottery that clays have a tendency either to fire whitish or reddish in oxidising conditions in the kiln, depending on how much iron they contain; but it is probable that medieval potters could achieve colours ranging from white to red from certain clay sources. Brooks (1980), in her study of some of the pottery from the Colstoun kiln site, noted quite a range in fabric colour from white to red, and there is no reason to believe that the potters used anything but the local, variable, boulder clay.

There is no clear evidence for the addition of temper to any of the pottery from Dundonald Castle. It is easier to imagine that the inclusions seen in the sherds were present in the source clay. It does not follow, however, that the less gritty fabrics are made from different clays than the more gritty ones. We may either be dealing with variable deposits or evidence that some potters sieved inclusions out, as, it is thought, did the potters of Throsk in the Forth Valley in the 17th century (Caldwell and Dean 1992, 28).

Differences in colour, hardness, grittiness and so on in the assemblage may reflect changing potting technology and fashions rather than different clay sources and production centres. We can perhaps detect a preference for fine pottery, especially jugs, which could be used as tableware, to be light coloured prior to the

14th century. It may be significant that some of the Red Gritty sherds have a white slip, perhaps to make them more acceptable to a market used to white wares. We might also detect a preference from the 14th century for the surfaces of pots to be smooth, even if the fabric itself was gritty. Later pottery appears thicker and clumsier, reflecting less skill on the part of the potters. Perhaps these potters were part-time, like those at Throsk in the 17th century, producing for a market where metal and wooden vessels were viewed as more effective alternatives to ceramic for many more tasks.

On the assumption that most of the Dundonald Castle pottery is local we can suggest that the sherds in Light and Red Gritty fabrics could come from the same production centre. There is no greater range of fabric here than comes from Colstoun. The Reduced Gritty Ware either demonstrates a significant change in potting technology or a preference for reduced wares. It is probable that these wares represent a different clay source.

The Smooth Ware fabrics would appear to represent yet another tradition where potters and/or customers valued a non-gritty fabric, possibly achieved by sieving the same clay source as was done by the makers of the white and red gritty wares. The division between fabrics (i) and (ii) may not be a particularly meaning-ful one, the two together representing a fabric with a broad range of colour.

Recent excavations by the Scottish Urban Archaeological Trust in Ayr, 13km down the coast, have demonstrated that the burgh was supplied with Light Gritty, Red Gritty and Reduced Ware pottery similar to that found at Dundonald Castle. No pottery similar to Smooth Ware fabric is reported from Ayr, but similar sherds (in the collections of the National Museums of Scotland) have been identified from Donald's Isle in Loch Doon in the south of Ayrshire, probably a 14th-century laird's dwelling. Pottery resembling Light Gritty and Red Gritty Wares has also been identified from the nearby motte at Kidsneuk (Watson 1918), and the castle at Auldhill, Portencross, a few miles up the coast (Caldwell *et al*. 1998, 57). Reduced Gritty pottery seems to be a widespread phenomenon in Scotland and it may require a scientific analytical technique to distinguish local variants.

Finally, it remains to comment on the forms of the vessels represented in the assemblage. Admittedly, its fragmentary nature makes identification of different forms difficult, but the preponderance of jugs has come to be expected from Scottish medieval sites: they probably served primarily for decanting wine or ale from casks, or fetching water for culinary purposes.

COINS

by David Caldwell

44   James III penny, class C. SF 15 [019].
45   James VI twopence (1623). SF 65 u/s.
46   Charles I turner (1632–9). SF 91 [001].
47   Charles II turner (1663). SF 119, u/s.
48   French jetton, 14th–15th century.

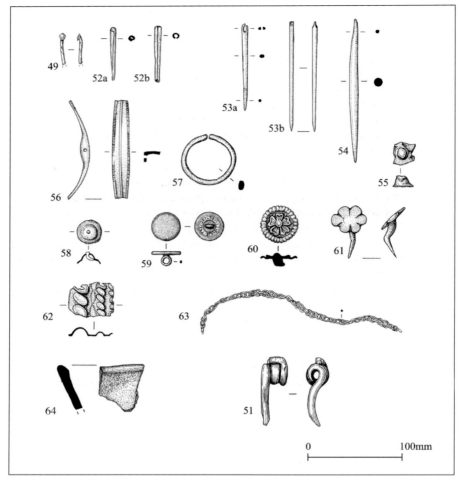

Fig 44 Metalwork of bronze and gold.

Metalwork (Figs 44 and 45)

by David Caldwell

49   Gold wire. Small scrap twisted and cut. Possibly scrap indicating fine metal-working on site as seen at Early Historic sites such as Dunollie (Alcock and Alcock 1987) and Dunadd (Lane and Campbell 2000) [409].

50   Ring (mounting), silver. SF 146 [757], Trench H, late 14th century.

51   Fibula Brooch pin and spring. Body of the brooch is missing, but this form of pin is characteristic of fibula brooches of the Romano-British period, copper alloy. SF 4 [018].

52   Lace chapes, copper alloy. SF 71 [506]. Gatehouse sequence: mid 15th century; SF 50 [177]. There are two other similar examples (unillustrated): SF 105 [727], Trench H, late 14th century; SF 97 [001].

53   Needles, copper alloy. SF 16 [019]; SF 79 [514]. Gatehouse sequence, early 14th century.

54   Awl, copper alloy. SF 9 [057].

55   Rivet, copper alloy. SF 35 [118].

56   Piece of a shoe buckle, copper alloy. [003(A)].

57   Ring mounting, copper alloy, e.g. for hanging curtains. SF 44.

58   Dome-shaped stud, copper alloy. SF 127 [918].

59   Button, copper alloy, disc-shaped with loop fastening and stamped inscription on its back: FREELE GILT STAND COLOR. Probably 19th century. SF 28 [003].

60   Button, copper alloy, with embossed design of a five-petalled flowerhead within a rope border. SF 151 [757], Trench H, late 14th century.

61   Stud mounting with six-petalled head, copper alloy. SF 53 [176].

62   Piece of decorative mounting with an embossed design, copper alloy. SF 111 [907].

63   Chain, copper alloy. In three pieces (one only illustrated), with a total length of about 370mm. The links are all formed of pieces of wire, butt-jointed. SF 75 [712], Trench H, c. 1550–1650.

64   Rim sherd of a cast bronze vessel. SF 72 [508] Gatehouse sequence, mid 15th century.

65   Fragments of copper alloy sheet metal. SF 37 [094].

66   Pointed iron ferrule. [757] Trench H, late 14th century.

67   Barbed iron arrowhead. London Museum, type 14: a type thought to have been used for hunting (1954, 70). SF 76 [707], Trench H, c. 1550.

68   Spearhead with narrow lozenge-section blade, iron with rivet hole in the socket. The relatively small blade form is charateristic of spears from 'Celtic or North British' settlement sites of the Early Historic period (Alcock 2003, 162–5), but they have also been recovered in Anglo-Saxon graves. SF 89 [124].

69   Spearhead with short, leaf-shaped blade, iron. The leaf-shaped blade can be compared with Early Historic spears from Buiston Crannog (Crone 2000, 145), and Edinburgh Castle (Driscoll and Yeoman 1997, 154–6), but can also be paraelled in Anglo-Saxon contexts. SF 38 [017].

70   Ring mounting, iron. SF 49 [001].

71   Tinder striker or fire steel (incomplete). Comparable to Early Historic example from Edinburgh Castle (Driscoll and Yeoman 1997, 154–6) SF 45 [144].

72   ?Chisel blade, iron. SF 57 [228].

73   Knife blade iron. The form of the blade with a stright back edge conforms to Laing's Type 3. It can be broadly dated to the Early Historic period as for instance at Buiston Crannog (Crone 2000, 145). SF 63 [311].

74   Portions of a iron chain, the links composed of bars with loops at each end. SF 154 [856].

75   Two iron knives and another iron implement from a matching set with bone handles. All three have whittle tangs and finely polished cylindrical grips finished at top and bottom with iron plates or washers. Their tops are decorated with base metal, denticulate mounts. The two knife blades, both

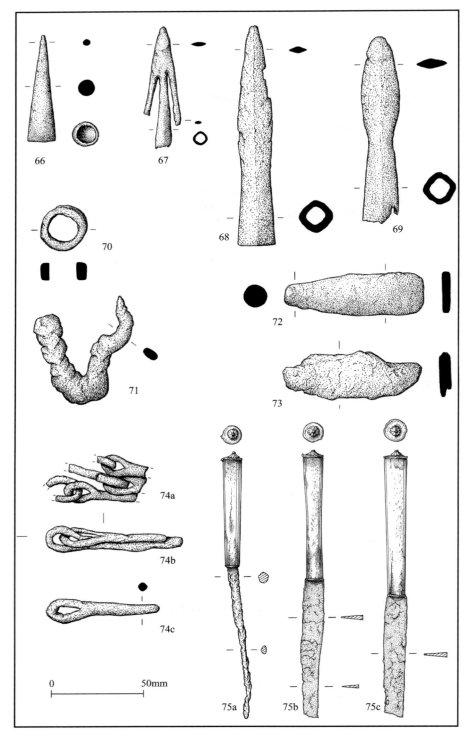

Fig 45 Ironwork.

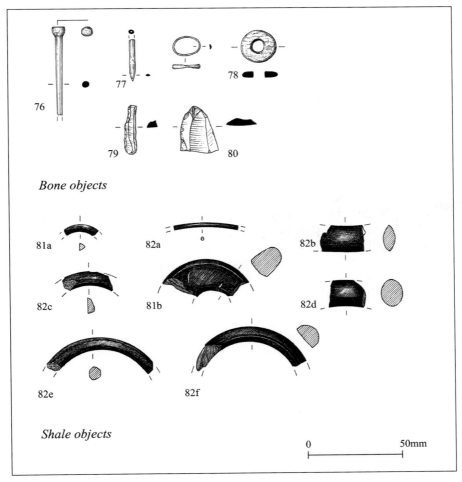

Bone objects

Shale objects

0   50mm

Fig 46 Bone and stone artefacts.

incomplete, are relatively narrow. The other implement, possibly a probe, has a long rounded blade. SF 68–70 [506], Gatehouse sequence, well fill, mid 15th century.

The form of the knife blades and the method of hafting with whittle tang and hilt plate suggest a 14th-century date for this set.

BONE OBJECTS (Fig 46)

by David Caldwell

76 Nail headed pin, incomplete. Iron Age (Stevenson 1955), and the MacKenzie Collection (Royal Museum of Scotland) SF 36 [118].
77 Piece of bone pin. Tip only. [138].
78 Disc-shaped bead. SF 88 [124].

OBJECTS OF STONE, SLATE, OIL SHALE AND
RELATED MATERIAL (Figs 46 and 47)

by Fraser Hunter

Dimensions are given in mm: L = length, W = width, H = height, D = diameter. Mass (M) is given in grams.

79　Blade made from black chert. Mesolithic type. SF 92 [162].

80　Blade made from honey-coloured flint. SF 98 [001].

81a　Finger-ring fragment, probably of D-section, shale. Polished to a high lustre all over; no remaining tool marks. Some wear, especially at top edge. L 18; W 3.5; H 3.5; M 0.2g; D 15–20 (26%). SF 25 [104].

81b　Broken ring-pendant? Broken ring with non-central perforation, polished to a low lustre all over. There is a hint of a shallower area at the narrowest part which may represent a deliberate groove for holding a thong (cf. Hay Fleming 1909, fig 21). The external edge retains traces of knife-trimming and abrasion; the perforation has vertical abrasion scars. L 46; W 19; H 13; M 8.6 g; D 20–25 (external D 55–60). SF 84, below [019]/[323].

82a　Lenticular-section bangle portion, shale. The outside more rounded than the inside; asymmetry in the internal surface suggests the centre was removed as a disc, worked preferentially from one side. Polished to a low lustre all over; internally, faint traces of vertical abrasion scratches survive. L 24.5; W 7; H 15; M 2.0g; D 50–55 (13%). SF 17 [018].

82b　Bangle fragment most likely of flattened D-section, shale. Depositional damage; the perforation bears faint diagonal abrasion scars. L 27.5; W 8; H 4; M 0.9g; D 40–55 (19%). SF 40 [156].

82c　Shale bangle fragment from Gatehouse sequence, mid 15th century. SF 66 [503].

82d　Small portion of a large shale bangle; diameter cannot be accurately measured. Oval in section, and polished to a high lustre. No visible tool marks. Trench H, late 14th century. L 20; W 15; H 12, M 4.4g. SF 121 [748].

82e　Portion of a large shale bangle with an irregular facetted finish. SF 139 [751].

82f　D-sectioned shale bangle portion with irregular slightly flattened faces. Polished to a low lustre. Externally, scratches in one area seem to post-date polishing and are perhaps an attempt to smooth the area after use-damage. Smoothed diagonal abrasion scars are visible in the perforation. L 58; W 8.5; H 13; M 7.8g; D 50–55 (40%). SF 43 [017].

83a　Spacer bead?, shale. SF 117 [841].

83b　Disc pendant, shale. Sub-circular disc with off-centre waisted perforation, D 7.5 mm. Both faces bear slight scratches, perhaps from use rather than manufacture; much of one face has flaked off although a slight smoothing of the fracture surface suggests that it saw continuing use. Smoothing of the edge has not completely removed the knife-cutting facets from shaping. The light weight means this cannot be a whorl, and the off-centre perforation implies it is a pendant rather than a bead. L 30.5; W 28; H 4.5; M 3.4g. SF 110 [840]:

84　Globular (incomplete) shale head of a pin or gaming piece? [042]/[052].

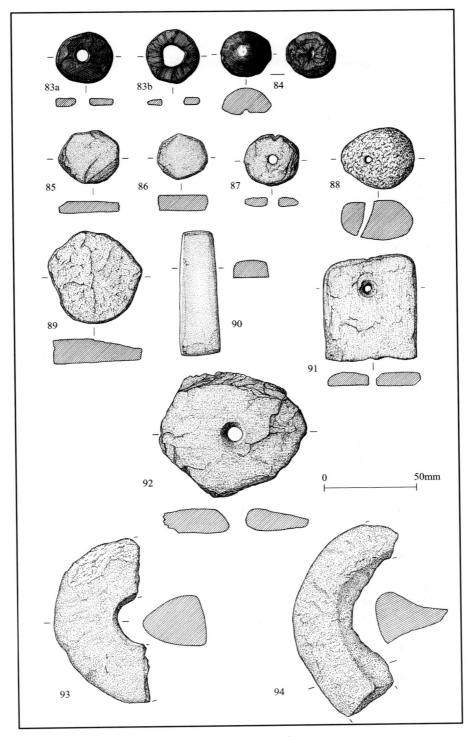

Fig 47 Objects of slate and stone.

Originally it would have been hemispherical with a flattened base preserved in one small area. and a cylindrical socket to hold a pin or peg (cf. Callander 1927, fig 5) but it has split at some 20° to the vertical. The outer surface is polished to a high lustre and irregularly rounded. The surviving part of the pin-hole is some 3.5mm diameter, terminating *c*. 10mm from the top of the dome. After breakage the item was reused: the fracture surface has a low lustre and the broken edges are rounded, probably from continuing use as a gaming counter. L 27; W 25.55; H 15; M 6.7g.

85   Slate disc, probably used as a playing piece. SF 147 [730].
86   Stone disc, playing piece. SF 140 [737], Trench H, late 14th century.
87   Shale spacer bead. SF 41 [123].
88   Pierced stone, weight. SF 33 [121].
89   Stone disc. [144].
90   Whetstone. SF 77 [707], Trench H, *c*. 1550.
91   Pierced stone weight? (incomplete). SF 13 [043].
92   Pierced stone weight? SF 80 [326].
93   Pierced stone weight? (incomplete). SF 136 [751].
94   Pierced stone weight? (incomplete). SF 7 [018].
95   Subrectangular stone with a shallow hollow worn in its top surface; not illustrated; 70 × 60 × 62mm. SF 56 [181].
96   Stone rubber?, not illustrated. Length 68mm. SF 159 [759], Trench H, late 14th century.

Discussion of Worked Stone Objects

Samples of oil shale were analysed by X-ray fluorescence (XRF) and X-radiography using standard methods, supplemented by visual inspection (Hunter *et al*. 1993; Davis 1993). They were grouped using each of the three methods, and the results were then reconciled to characterise the raw materials and identify any exotic elements as far as possible.

The Dundonald assemblage of objects of shale and related materials is typical of Iron Age/Early Historic assemblages in areas where the raw material is abundant, with a diverse range of artifacts dominated by bangles. Bangles of jet-like material are known from the early Bronze Age to the Norse period. They have largely evaded attempts to construct a meaningful typology, although most are later prehistoric or Early Historic. For local parallels see Auldhill (Hunter 1998) and Carwinning (Cowie 1978). The lenticular bangle (no. 82, SF 17) bears some resemblance to a small number of thin, tall bangles dating to the later 1st millennium AD (Hunter 1998, 50, fig 19.7), but the similarity is not close enough to press the dating too far. Simple finger-rings similar to no. 81 (SF 25) are known from the Iron Age (e.g. Dunagoil 'flute', Mann 1925, 135) to the Norse period (e.g. Jarlshof, Shetland: Hamilton 1956, fig 56) and cannot be more tightly dated.

The socketed gaming piece (no. 84) is the most interesting item in the assemblage. Such items occur in bone as well as jet-like materials, and their use has been much debated. Stevenson classes them as pin-heads (1955, 292–3), but Close-Brooks suggests their flattened bases and on occasions multiple occurrence point to use as pegged gaming pieces (1986, 166); this is supported by a number of Irish sets of related items (e.g. Raftery 1983, 231, no. 619). The suggested secondary use of the Dundonald example as a counter would support use as a gaming piece, and this interpretation seems most plausible.

If no. 81 (SF 84) is indeed a ring pendant, it finds both later Iron Age and Early Historic parallels. There are Iron Age examples from Cairngryfe (Lanarkshire) and Traprain Law (East Lothian) (Childe 1941, pl. LII; Curle and Cree 1921, 198, fig 24.15–16), while one from a long cist at St Andrews (Hay Fleming 1909, fig 21) extends the dating into the early historic period. There are also Roman-period examples from the Hadrian's Wall zone at Housesteads, South Shields and Carvoran, the last a Scottish import (Allason-Jones and Miket 1984, no. 7.107; Allason-Jones and Jones 1994, 269). The full distribution of such items has never been mapped, though an example from Meare (Somerset) indicates that it is not solely a northern type (Gray and Bulleid 1953, 268, fig 64). While ring-pendants are characterised by the presence of a groove to hold a thong, simple disc pendants like no. 83b (SF 110) and perhaps no. 83a (SF 117) are also readily paralleled in Iron Age and early historic contexts (e.g. Munro 1882, fig 28; Nisbet 1996, fig 11/CM949).

The two unfinished items are clear evidence of on-site working of the material. The absence of large quantities of working debris (which invariably accompanies the working of such materials due to the frequency of breakages) suggests the production focus was elsewhere on the site or was not recognised on excavation, as is often the case. The working of cannel coal and shale is typical of Ayrshire sites of Iron Age/early historic date (Hunter 1998, 51–2), on account of the local abundance of raw material sources.

In summary, Dundonald presents a diverse and interesting assemblage, all of which can be accommodated in an Iron Age–Early Historic framework, but little of which is more diagnostic. Only the socketed gaming piece provides a more specific dating bracket of the 2nd to 7th century AD. Most of the material is local canneloid shales which were worked on site, but there were also a few more exotic items reaching the site which were more highly valued, and attempts were made to reuse these when they broke. This presents a valuable case study of this little-studied material type.

INSCRIBED AND ENGRAVED SLATES (Figs 48 and 49)

by David Caldwell

The excavations produced a surprisingly rich collection of fragments of slate with graffiti. It is likely that these slates were originally intended as roofing material and a few of them show signs of holes having been cut through them for pegging them on a roof. These designs on these slates have evidently been incised with a metal point. In recent years several important discoveries of inscribed slates from the Middle Ages have been made in the west of Scotland. A collection of slates including inscriptions and motif pieces was excavated at St Blane's, Bute, in the late 19th century (Anderson 1900) and more recently at the site of a monastery on Inchmarnock, Bute (DES 2001, 22), which are both of Early Historic date, while a late medieval group recovered during the cleaning of the main drain of Paisley

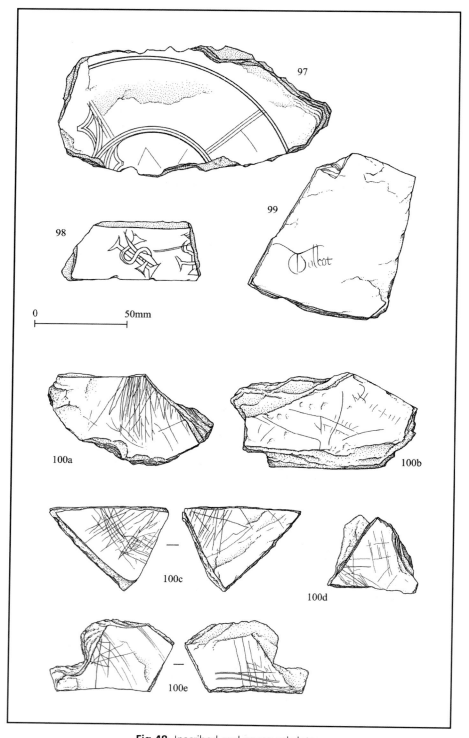

Fig 48 Inscribed and engraved slates.

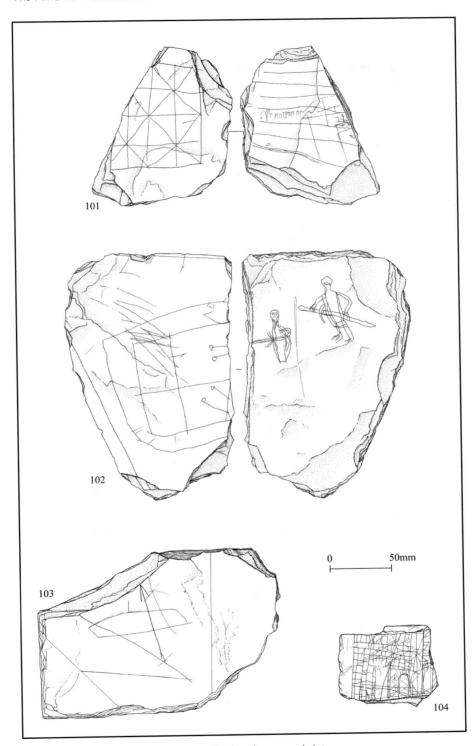

Fig 49 Inscribed and engraved slates.

Abbey includes scraps of poetry and the earliest musical notation to survive in Scotland (Malden 2000, 199–208). These inscribed slates from Dundonald are particularly noteworthy for having been recovered from a secular site and all appear to date to the later Middle Ages.

97 Trial piece with bold, compass-drawn tracery design. SF 120.
98 Fragment with the 'IHS' monogram drawn twice in bold capitals. SF 93 [727], Trench H, late 14th century.
99 Fragment of roof slate (an adjoining piece has a nail hole) engraved 'Talbot' in a neat hand with a Lombardic capital 'T'. SF 1 [004]. 'Talbot' might either be a type of hunting dog or an English surname. Nobody with the name Talbot is known to have had any association with the castle.
100 Five incised fragments. One has a very faint – or rubbed out? – inscription, possibly 'Jacobus'. SF 158 [759], Trench H, late 14th century.
101 Fragment of slate, one side ruled for writing and with a very faint inscription, possibly 'In nomine …' The other side has an incomplete gaming board for a game like chess or draughts. SF 138 [715], Trench H, c. 1450–c. 1550.
102 Fragment with crude engravings on one side of two men with swords with down turned quillons characteristic of Scottish medieval swords. The other side has a rectangular pattern, perhaps a gaming board. Along one of the broken edges are what may be the feet and legs of two 'match-stick' men. SF 116 [907].
103 Slate with a drawing of a bow and arrow. SF 2 [004].
104 Fragment with a drawing of a building. [003].

In addition, a number of slates with less involved marking were recovered: SF 10 [052]; SF 107 [905]; SF 101 [720]; SF 103 [727]; SF 112 [907]; SF 113 [163]; SF 6 [023]; SF 102 [727]. These are not illustrated.

GLASSWORK (Fig 50)

by David Caldwell

105 Blue glass bead. [067].
106 Biconical bead, opaque green glass. Guido's type 5iv dating from the 6th to 7th centuries (1999, 44) SF 137 [746].
107 Bottle seal with the initials 'GH'. SF 27 [003].
108 Blue glass bead, possibly wound. SF 96 [001].
109 Melon Bead, blue glass with ridged decoration. Dates to 1st to 2nd century AD (Guido 1978, 100). SF 148 [758].

CLAY PIPES

by Dennis Gallagher

Twenty-two fragments of clay pipe were recovered from twelve different contexts. Most of the fragments are of 19th-century or later date. Pipes by William White of Glasgow are predominant amongst the modern stems, although there is one more local product by Robert Carty of Ayr. The business of Carty and Hamilton was

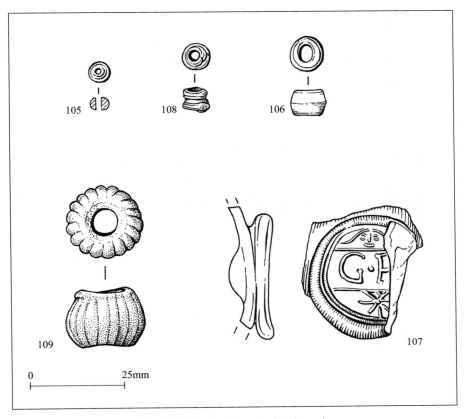

Fig 50 Glass beads and a bottle seal.

active in Ayr from 1857 until 1900, and it continued from 1900 to 1935 as Robert Carty & Co. (Martin 1987, 174). The fragment present in this assemblage may date from the later period.

There is one example of a pre-19th-century bowl in the assemblage. This is a Tyneside product of *c*. 1680–1710 (Edwards 1988, 9).

5   Scientific Studies

ANIMAL BONES

by Jennifer Thoms

The bones were identified to element and species in the Department of Archaeology and Prehistory, Sheffield University. The assemblage mainly comprised sheep bones although other domesticates and non-domesticates were present. The bones were largely complete and in very good condition. The sheep bones were analysed for information on age at death, and all bones were examined for fragmentation, preservation and butchery information. It was discovered that very few of the bones had been butchered. The age at death data seemed to suggest that most of the sheep had been butchered very young.

The results were then compared with some other contemporaneous sites in Scotland. It was hoped that the analysis of the animal bones might provide some information about the animal husbandry practices and the dietary preferences of the late 15th to mid 16th century in this part of Scotland.

A number of hypotheses are forwarded on the circumstances and/or animal management régimes that may have led to this unusual assemblage.

It was further hoped that the archaeozoological analysis might shed some light on the functions of the room from which the bone assemblage was recovered. From the archaeological evidence this appears to be a pit prison, which has been converted by the addition of a revetted floor into some sort of store room.

The bones were identified to element and species by comparison with modern defleshed specimens and archaeological comparative material in the reference collection of the Department of Archaeology and Prehistory in the University of Sheffield.

Each individual bone was examined carefully using a magnifying glass and a strong light. They were examined for signs of gnawing by dogs and rodents and for any knife marks. The knife marks were classified according to type following Binford (1981).

Results

The following species were identified in the faunal remains; horse (*Equus* sp.), cattle (*Bos taurus*), pig (*Sus* sp.), sheep (*Ovis aries*), dog (*Canis familiaris*), domestic cat (*Felis catus*), hare (*Lepus* sp.), rabbit (*Oryctolagus cuniculus*), badger (*Meles meles*), polecat (*Mustela putorius*), possible wildcat (*Felis silvestris*) and possible fox (*Vulpes vulpes*).

Interpretation

It was decided to treat all the contexts as belonging to one phase, dating from the 15th to 16th century AD. As it seemed likely from the good condition of the bones that the deposits had been laid down over a short period of time no attempt was made to analyse the bones from each context individually. This decision was validated by the observation that some bones from the same individual animal were found in more than one context. For example, most of the badger bones were retrieved from [103], but a left humerus, left radius and a left ulna were retrieved from [100]. Similarly a likely matching pair of cat femurs (same fusion state and size) were retrieved from [100] and [104], and a probable matching pair of cat humeri were retrieved from [101] and [104].

It would seem likely therefore that the contexts were either all deposited at around the same time or that they experienced subsequent mixing. In either case it is sensible to treat the bones as coming from one phase of deposition.

It can be further speculated that the bones were not subjected to any erosion processes, as they showed little sign of abrasion or fragmentation.

It can be seen that the main domesticated species are represented: horse, cattle, pig, sheep, dog, and cat. Some of these animals were identified on the basis of only one bone. One second phalanx was identified as horse, and one femur was recognised as pig.

Four species which are not today considered domesticates are also present: hare, badger, fox, and wildcat. The polecat was represented by one fragment of skull, and the putative wildcat by one complete right tibia. It is not possible to distinguish between polecat and its domesticated counterpart, the ferret, from the bone fragment retrieved from Dundonald (Andrew Kitchener, pers. comm.). The possibility exists that the possible wildcat is a domestic cat, but if so it is peculiarly massive in stature. Similarly, the possibility that the fox is in fact a gracile domestic dog cannot be ruled out.

An insight into the animal management practices is revealed by the age of death evidence. Together the mandibular and fusion evidence appear to suggest that most (>65%) of the animals were killed very young (<1 year old). This does not suggest the exploitation of the sheep for wool, as sheep produce little wool in their first year of life. Also, they have not reached their optimum age for meat, as such primitive breeds raised in a non-intensive manner are unlikely to have attained their maximum weight by this age. It could be speculated that the sheep might have been killed before they had attained their maximum weight if circumstances made it necessary to make the most efficient use of the resources available. Rearing of livestock for meat is a very inefficient way to use land (Speth 1989). Both dairying and crop production are better use of resources. The sheep at Dundonald may represent animals which have been killed before attaining maximum body weight because of stresses on their food resources. An example of such a stress might be a shortage of winter fodder, or the need to convert pasture land to arable.

Perhaps some sort of disaster, such as disease, may have necessitated the slaughter of a large proportion of the herd. An event such as this, where most or all of the herd are slaughtered at one time, would be expected to show peaks of deaths approximately one year apart. Unfortunately both the mandibular and the epiphyseal fusion periods cover such long periods of time that such detailed information cannot be determined from them.

Alternatively the sheep may have been killed younger than was economically most productive because there was no need to optimise resources. The consumption of younger animals suggests that there was not much concern for maximising their resource exploitation and this might also explain the absence of signs of marrow extraction from the bones.

Conclusions

The bones were in a remarkably good state of preservation with few showing signs of fragmentation, or gnawing. When compared to contemporaneous Scottish sites for which data are available the assemblage from Dundonald Castle appears to be unique in a number of ways. The bones are much less fragmented than those retrieved from other sites, with comparatively few displaying any signs of butchery marks or gnawing by dogs or rodents. Sheep comprised a very much larger proportion of the assemblage than they did at either Edinburgh or Rattray castles, or indeed the urban sites for which comparative figures are available.

It seems highly unlikely that this assemblage is typical of sites of similar age in western lowland Scotland. It would therefore seem imprudent to draw any general conclusions about animal husbandry in the area, or the dietary preferences of the site's occupants. The age-at-death information suggests that the majority of sheep (65.4%) were killed in their first year of life, which does not suggest an economy based on the production of either milk, meat or wool (Payne 1973). However, due to the relatively small flock size (around 33 individuals), this figure represents only about 22 sheep, while the flock studied by Payne (1973), on which the meat, milk and wool curves are based, comprised 147 individuals.

The assemblage is unusual in that the bones are largely complete and very well preserved. In these respects it differs from other medieval assemblages which tend to be well fragmented and acutely butchered. A few other animals are present: a horse is represented by one phalanx, and a pig by one femur. The cattle bones appear to represent butchery waste, being fragmented and containing a number of chopping and other butchery marks.

The bones of a number of non-domesticates were also retrieved from the site. As these do not represent many individual animals, it is possible they are accidental inclusions, the animals perhaps having fallen into the chamber or having entered in search of food or a place to die.

It would appear that this assemblage, being so unusual and atypical of medieval faunal remains, does not shed much light on the animal husbandry practices or the dietary preferences of the 15th to 16th century in lowland west Scotland. It may represent a one-off event, possibly the result of unusual hardship, which necessitated the killing of a number of sheep before they were economically useful. Alternatively the presence of so many young sheep in the assemblage may indicate wealth and opulence, inferring that there was no need to kill the sheep at their most productive age but that young, tender meat could be enjoyed.

The part of the assemblage which has resulted from human activity does not represent intensive or efficient use of the animal resource. The majority of the animals have been killed at too young an age to have produced much, if any, wool. They are unlikely, similarly, to have achieved their optimum meat-bearing weight, yet have been kept alive longer than would conventionally be regarded as normal for a dairying economy (cf. McCormick 1992).

The second aim of the research was to attempt to find out about the possible function of the chamber in which the animal remains were found.

Perhaps the most likely explanation for the presence of these animal bones in the chamber is that the assemblage represents domestic waste: animals that had been butchered and eaten. The material may have lain in a primary disposal site, such as a kitchen floor, for a short while, when the bones may have been gnawed by dogs. This material may then have been moved to a dump site, perhaps a midden or a disused, collapsing room of the castle. At this stage the anomalous pig and horse bones may have been added (remnants of earlier refuse on the dump site, perhaps). The bones may have ended up in the vault, along with masonry and rubble, as part of a tidying operation.

PLANT REMAINS

by Tim Holden

Methodology

The environmental samples were processed using a system of flotation and wet sieving. The floating debris (the flot) was collected in sieves of mesh sizes 0.3mm and 1mm and the non-floating residue (the retent) was wet-sieved through a 1mm mesh. All flot material above 1mm was sorted by trained technicians using binocular microscopes and any items of archaeological or ecological interest were removed for later identification. All retent material was sorted by eye or with the use of a low-powered magnifying lens and again any items of interest routinely removed. Identifications were made using modern comparative material from the collection of AOC (Scotland) Ltd.

The Charred Plant Remains

The charred plant remains were recovered from a number of negative features associated with Structures 1, 3 and 4 which are considered to be of Iron Age or Early Medieval date. Preservation of the remains was generally poor because of the charring conditions and the post-depositional environment. As a result of this a proportion of the identifications remain tentative. The diversity of the plant remains are not great so it has not been possible to highlight any form of context-related activity. However, this analysis has provided additional information regarding aspects of the site economy and sediment formation processes.

Modern contamination in the form of uncarbonised seeds can be demonstrated for a number of samples indicating some downward movement of particles through the profile, probably by earthworm activity. These are primarily the nutlets of the common stinging nettle or other species indicative of waste ground and are of little diagnostic value in themselves.

The carbonised plant remains are dominated by three classes of material, cereal grains, 'weed seeds' (used in its general sense) and nut shell fragments.

Cereal Grains

The remains of three major cereal staples have been recovered, barley, oats and wheat. In all cases it was the grains alone (i.e. with no chaff remains) that were recovered.

Many of the barley grains were in a poor state of preservation but a number did enable the identification of the hulled variety and it seems likely that most of the poorly preserved grains are also of this type. Hulled barley has been a component of British agriculture since the Neolithic (e.g. Hillman 1981, Bond 1994, Fairweather and Ralston 1993) but it becomes particularly prevalent in the Iron Age and later periods. It has been recovered from numerous locations on the Scottish mainland where it commonly replaces the naked barley which dominated previously (e.g. Greig 1991, van der Veen 1985, Carter and Holden 2000). Hulled barley is a typical component of charred Iron Age and Early Medieval plant assemblages and is therefore quite in keeping with the proposed dating of Structures 1, 3 and 4.

Small numbers of oat grains were recovered from five contexts but without the presence of the diagnostic chaff fragments it is impossible to be more specific regarding their identification. Given the likely Iron Age/Early Medieval date of the contexts concerned and the high concentration of oats relative to weeds of cultivation it is, however, likely that they represent the remains of a cereal crop: either *Avena strigosa* (bristle oat), or *Avena sativa* (common oat). Both of these oat species are known from at least the Roman period in Scotland (Boyd 1988), but it is the bristle oat which tends to dominate most of the early finds. The bristle oat, however, was gradually replaced by the more productive common oat, such that today it only survives as a crop in the most exposed locations in the Northern Isles (e.g. Hinton 1990).

Wheat grain was recovered from a total of six contexts. As with the oats, none of the more diagnostic chaff fragments was recovered, but on the basis of grain morphology the grain can be divided into two distinct categories. There are those with a plump rounded appearance typical of *Triticum aestivo-compactum* (bread/compact wheat) and those with a drop-like shape viewed from the dorsal surface and with a high back of maximum depth at a point just behind the embryo when viewed laterally. These grains are more typical of *Triticum dicoccum* (emmer wheat). Both emmer and bread wheats have been recovered from Northern Britain sometimes being found together such as at the Neolithic site of Balbridie (Grampian) (Fairweather and Ralston 1993). Although bread wheat generally tends to replace emmer in the later periods it is well documented for the Iron Age and occasional finds are also reported from Medieval contexts (Boyd 1988). In view of this it would not be unprecedented to find emmer in the Dundonald samples. However, there is very good evidence from the excavation report of charcoal-rich layers of Neolithic date (*c.* 5000 BP) underlying later structures. It is also clear that in the construction of levelling deposits during the Iron Age and Medieval period there has been large-scale reworking of earlier deposits. It is therefore possible that, even though the charred assemblages from Structures 1, 3 and 4 are essentially Iron-Age or later in date (as supported by the presence of hulled barley and oats) that some of the wheat actually derives from earlier, Neolithic sources.

Conclusions

The plant remains present a picture in which a mixed assemblage of clean grain has become charred in the absence of any of its associated chaff. There may be a taphonomic reason for the apparent absence of chaff but the evidence, based upon identifications from fifteen small samples, suggests that a clean grain product had become charred. This could be explained as an accumulation of grain lost into the fire during small scale processing, possibly grain drying or food preparation. In the absence of more comprehensive sampling, however, it is not possible to rule out the possibility that these represent the residual remains of grain burnt elsewhere on the site during large scale corn drying or in a conflagration of, for example, a storage facility.

THERMOLUMINESCENCE DATING RESULTS

by David Sanderson

Summary

The possibility of utilising thermoluminescence dating at Dundonald Castle was discussed during the excavations in the late 1980s and a field trip to record environmental dose rates was arranged. A small series of samples comprising a burned clay material and several heated stones were then submitted for analysis. The material was analysed in 1989, eventually producing six age estimates based on the additive-dose feldspar inclusion method. Here the samples dated and the measurements conducted are summarised. The precision obtained from these samples was somewhat disappointing.

The heated stones had very low internal radioactivity levels, leading to high fractional uncertainties in assessed dose rates. The burned clay/daub material by contrast had very high porosity leading to uncertainties in past water contents, which also resulted in high uncertainties in dose rates. Nonetheless the demonstration that burned clay/daub could be used for dating is itself of interest. Moreover the results confirm the presence of late Bronze Age or early Iron Age activity on the site, together with later iron age phases and the expected later medieval activities.

Samples

Table 1 summarises the samples submitted to the laboratory by Gordon Ewart in November 1988 together with a paraphrase of the chronological significance of the work, taken from the submission forms.

Measurements

The samples were analysed using the additive-dose feldspar inclusion thermoluminescence (TL) method. Sample preparation comprised measurement of actual and saturated water contents (required for dose rate assessment), removal of surface material, and preparation of feldspar separates from the interior portions of each sample, which were also used for dose rate measurement by thick-source

Table 1 Samples submitted and their associated questions

Laboratory reference	Sample description	Context	Significance
SUTL107	Ceramic – pottery scatter or collapsed kiln lining	DC88 2005	Part of complex of 'Hearth associated activity'; should date primary hut construction at the E end of the site
SUTL108	Fired-clay lined pit	DC88 892	The pit is sealed by major levelling and metalling of the site; in turn associated with 'dark age' stonework. Thus the date should provide a *terminus ante-quem* for stone building on the site and a *post-quem* for the late iron age period
SUTL109	Burnt daub	DC88 966	Arguably post-dates the wars of independence and may predate the late 14th century reconstruction; alternatively may be associated with later 15th or 16th century activity
SUTL110, 111	Domestic hearth	DC87 243	From an eroded part of the site, containing 15th and 16th century material, but potentially of 13th century or earlier age
SUTL112,113	Domestic hearth	DC87 103	Secondary hearth in a position that associates with a series of badly damaged timber and stone structures
SUTL114,115	Domestic hearth	DC87 043	Apparently central hearth in main room of '14th century' domestic range; aim of dating is to identify the late use of the much damaged stone hall, originally built in the 12th century, but finally subdivided *c.* 1450
SUTL116,117	Domestic hearth	DC87 135	Context could date from dark age to medieval periods; aim of dating is to help define a stratified sequence of general levels in the highest part of the hill

beta counting (Sanderson 1988a) and neutron activation analysis. Gamma ray dose rates to define the radiation environment of the samples had been recorded on-site during the 1988 excavation season. The feldspar fractions were separated from sieved material (90–125 microns) following sample disaggregation, using a series of heavy liquids (sodium polytungstate solutions prepared at densities of 2.52, 2.58, 2.62 and 2.74g ml^{-1}) and a centrifuge. The resulting density separates were treated in HCl and dilute HF to remove carbonates and etch the grain surfaces prior to deposition on 0.25mm thick stainless-steel discs for TL measurement.

The TL measurement sequence followed an additive sequence to determine the radiation dose experienced since last firing, utilising a similar approach to that developed for analysis of vitrified forts in the mid 1980s (Sanderson *et al.* 1988). Each sample was split into eight aliquots which were irradiated to known added doses using a calibrated ^{90}Sr source prior to recording TL at 5°C s^{-1} heating rates up to 500°C. Four measurement cycles were followed. In the first cycle the natural signal (derived from the archaeological exposure) plus added dose was measured; the second TL cycle regenerated a signal in the laboratory to investigate the low-dose linearity and sensitivity changes experienced by the sample. The third measurement was in response to a fixed laboratory dose, used to normalise the response from each sub-sample, In the fourth measurement cycle half the sample discs were irradiated prior to storage for a 6–8 week period in the dark to monitor fading. At the end of the storage period the other set of discs was also irradiated, and all discs measured together. Prior to each TL measurement cycle the samples were heated overnight at 135°C in an attempt to remove unstable TL signal components (Sanderson 1988b) induced by the laboratory irradiations that might interfere with dating signals in the 300–500°C temperature region.

The TL measurements thus took place over a period of several months, with the sample preparation and initial readings being undertaken over a 2–3 week period, followed by fading tests and age assessment. Data analysis included determination of the TL plateau temperature range (Aitken 1985), stored dose estimate and its precision, sensitivity changes and fading properties. The dose rates determined from *in situ* gamma spectrometry, beta counting (Sanderson 1988a) and neutron activation analysis were used together with water content data and cosmic ray dose rates (Prescott and Stephan 1982) to model the effective dose rates to the sample (Aitken 1983). The TL ages and their uncertainties were then calculated as the quotient of stored dose over dose rate (Aitken 1985).

Results

Tables 2 and 3 summarise the luminescence results and dose rates assessments based on the original laboratory records from the time. It is perhaps worth reviewing the data and commenting on them. The TL data used to estimate stored dose are shown in Table 2, which gives details of the temperature range and quality of the 'plateau' (i.e. the temperature range over which the stored dose estimate was considered constant within measurement error), the proportion of the stored dose accounted for by supralinearity (represented by the ratio of the second glow dose response curve intercept, I, and the palaeodose P), the sensitivity change observed between first and second heatings of the sample, the result of the fading test, and the estimated stored dose. As can be seen the samples exhibited diverse behaviour leading to variable quality of stored dose determination. Three samples showed plateau variations of better than ±5% (SUTL107, 108b, 114); the others having data sets with approximately 10% variations across the high temperature TL region. Supralinearity was generally small compared with measurement errors. Samples SUTL111 and 115 (hearth stones) showed marked sensitivity changes between first and second heatings and produced fading test results that implied increasing signals following dark storage, albeit at low precision. The other samples give very satisfactory results in fading tests, and in sensitivity change behaviour. The stored dose estimates range from 3.7 to 7.3 Gy

Table 2 Luminescence measurements and stored dose estimates

Laboratory reference	Grain size /μm	Density /g ml^{-1}	Plateau Range /°C	Variation /%	Supralinearity I/P ratio	1st/2nd glow Slope ratio	Fading test Remnant TL	Stored dose /Gy
SUTL107	90–125	2.51–2.58	340–430	2.3%	0±0.04	1.07±0.19	1.00±0.02	7.32±0.63
SUTL108a	90–125	2.51–2.58	390–430	12.1%	-0.10±0.12	0.68±0.09	1.00±0.05	4.33±0.92
SUTL108b	90–125	2.28–2.62	360–420	4.1%	-0.17±0.12	0.88±0.05	0.96±0.04	3.67±0.21
SUTL111	90–125	2.62–2.74	400–450	10.7%	0.01±0.14	2.39±0.49	1.34±0.14	1.17±0.25
SUTL114	90–125	2.58–2.62	390–430	1.9%	0.19±0.03	0.80±0.02	0.94±0.05	0.85±0.11
SUTL115	90–125	2.62–2.74	360–390	9.2%	0.23±0.14	1.54±0.25	1.36±0.06	0.56±0.22

Table 3 Dose rate measurements and luminescence age estimates

Laboratory reference	Water content %	Beta dose by TSBC mGy a^{-1}	Beta dose rate by NAA No Rn	Full series	Gamma and cosmic dose rate mGy a^{-1}	Total effective dose rate mGy a^{-1}	Age ka BP	TL date Years AD/BC
SUTL107	40±30	2.14±0.14	2.04±0.16	2.36±0.17	0.57±0.04	2.43±0.34	3.02±0.49	1030±490 BC
SUTL108a	30±30	1.16±0.12	1.36±0.04	1.59±0.06	0.62±0.4	1.99±0.52	2.17±0.73	180±730 BC
SUTL108b	50±50	0.82±0.11	1.36±0.06	1.59±0.07	0.62±0.4	1.55±0.45	2.37±0.7	380±700 BC
SUTL111	2±2	1.68±0.13	1.3±0.16	1.40±0.16	0.46±0.04	1.90±0.21	0.62±0.21	1370±150 AD
SUTL114	3±2	0.46±0.08	0.25±0.04	0.31±0.04	0.52±0.04	1.15±0.19	0.74±0.15	1250±150 AD
SUTL115	3±2	0.35±0.08	0.55±0.07	0.61±0.07	0.53±0.04	0.93±0.14	0.60±0.25	1390±250 AD

for the ceramic samples, down to approximately 1 Gy or less for the younger hearthstone samples.

Table 3 presents the dose rate analysis and age estimates, again reproducing the data held in the original laboratory records. It is notable that the water contents of the ceramic samples are much higher than for the hearthstones, and that those assessed for the daub samples are higher than for the pottery or kiln lining material. The uncertainties associated with the past water content have been assessed as 75–100% of the assumed values. For the hearthstones, which have low saturated water contents, taking such values has little impact on dating precision. But for the more porous ceramic samples the uncertainty of the water content estimate has a significant impact on dating precision. Beta dose rates were estimated for the dry matrix by both TSBC and NAA, as indicated above. The correspondence is quite good, the NAA based estimates being tabulated both on the assumption of total radon retention and total radon loss for the uranium decay series. The gamma and cosmic ray dose rates are also shown. For some reason the uncertainty associated with sample SUTL108 appears to be very much higher than for the other samples. This together with the high water content uncertainty leads to the high errors associated with the dates from these two samples.

Discussion

The TL dates obtained were of disappointing precision for the reasons outlined in the previous section. Nonetheless they follow a sensible chronological sequence relative to what was known or believed about the samples at time of collection. As indicated above, the uncertainties in the age calculations arise from the combination of many sources. Taken at face value the date assigned to SUTL107 is consistent with a late bronze age or early iron age attribution. Those from sample SUTL108 appear to sit better with a pre-Roman Iron age than first millennium AD period, although with the errors as originally assessed, it is hard to distinguish between these two cases. The later hearthstone results are also consistent with the archaeological sequence, but lack the necessary precision to help to resolve the interesting but challenging questions associated with the structural sequence in the medieval period.

These data were part of a sequence of approximately 200 samples examined from Scottish archaeological sites between 1986 and 1989 using the feldspar inclusion method. Lamentably few of these data have been published, although it is to be hoped that this will eventually take place as the excavation reports are completed. The use of burnt daub as a dating material is interesting, although obtaining more precise results in future work will depend on achieving closer estimates of the past water content history of samples than available in these analyses. In reviewing these old data, collected within the first two years of luminescence dating work conducted in East Kilbride, it is tempting to consider whether re-analysis of the old data sets, or perhaps of retained material might perhaps result in better age estimates. The original TL data were measured manually, using a very laborious procedure in comparison with the automated approaches adopted today. Laboratory records show that the TL determinations from those samples for which ages were estimated were in fact replicated on more than one mineral phase following review of the initial data from all eleven samples originally prepared. The decision not to pursue these other determinations to age estimation was based on the low signal levels obtained in their runs, plus a recognition of the problems of the high water content matrices (the samples actually dispersed in water during saturated water content measurement) and the low dose rates obtained from the hearthstones. A further concern related to the possible effects of disaggregating hard rocks like the basic basaltic rocks encountered here. However Strickertsson *et al.* (1998) did investigate the effect of so called 'brutal disaggregation' on TL signals from the vitrified material from Dundonald and concluded that such materials could in fact be used.

Today much of the work of the laboratory is associated with dating sediments. These not only show high saturated water contents (as in the burnt clay samples), but also frequently have low internal dose rates such as those encountered in the Dundonald hearths. Using contemporary procedures it may be possible to obtain higher precision age estimates from material of this sort that originally envisaged. At the time it was thought more appropriate to concentrate effort on higher dose-rate samples from other lithologies (such as for example the hearthstones from Tofts Ness and Dunion Hill, which were successfully dated). It may however be worth reviewing retained samples and outstanding archaeological questions at Dundonald in a consideration as to whether the technical improvements of the last twenty years have changed the potential outlook for dating materials of this sort.

6   Discussion and Interpretation

In considering the results of the excavations, one factor should be borne in mind. The excavation was concentrated almost entirely on those parts of the site enclosed by the late medieval barmkin wall. With the exception of the six trial trenches on the site of the Period 4 E gatehouse, excavation was limited to a small part of the Castle Hill, and did not investigate the entire sequence of fortification at Dundonald. No excavation was carried out on the area to the W of the Period 6 tower-house, nor at any point on any of the lower terraces. However, despite its great complexity a phased chronology of the site emerged (Figs 8 and 51).

The results confirm the long history of Dundonald, permitting assumptions to be made about other parts of the castle during each successive phase of occupation. Indeed one of the merits of concentrating on one crucial part of the site, in this instance the highest point of the natural hill, was the demonstration of the changing focus for the twin roles of residence and fortress.

During Period 2, the archaeological evidence would appear to suggest that Dundonald was more intensively occupied than in any subsequent phase. Some of the lacunae in the excavated evidence from Periods 4 and 6, however, when it would have ranked among the most important castles in Scotland, may simply reflect the chances of survival. Whatever the reason, it was still something of a surprise to discover that much of the area enclosed by at least two phases of medieval lime-mortared ramparts also contained evidence of an earlier fortress.

Dundonald may now be considered alongside early historic fortresses like Dunadd (Argyll), Dunollie (Argyll) and the Mote of Mark (Kirkcudbrightshire), and with the classic 13th-century enclosure castles of Bothwell (Lanarkshire), Caerlaverock (Dumfriesshire), and Kildrummy (Aberdeenshire). The continuity of territorial context and consequent patterns of lordship are central to understanding the sequence of occupation on the site.

PERIOD 1 (*c*. 1500–*c*. 500 BC)

The isolated nature of the Period 1 evidence is a consequence of the extent of the Period 2a settlement, which appears to have removed traces of earlier occupation. The pottery scatter, which provided a date of 1030 ± 490 BC, coupled with the kiln-like structures all suggest a permanent settlement. Successive phases of settlement created areas of disturbed and even inverted stratigraphy. The builders of the later Period 2 structures removed traces of earlier buildings in order to clear an appropriate area for each house site, with the exception of the slightly sloping area at the extreme north-east of Trench B. At this point on the hill, fragmentary Period 1 evidence survived below a building platform. Environmental evidence (see pp. 115–17) confirms the general dating parameters for a Bronze Age presence, for example, with the incidence of emmer wheat.

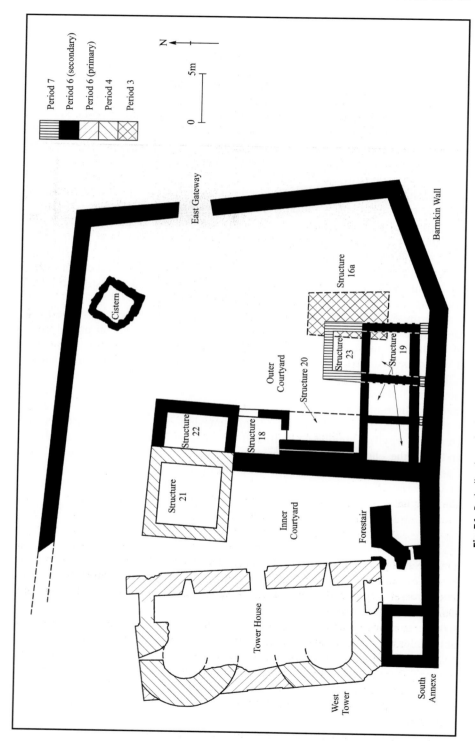

Fig 51 Periodisation of principal buildings within barmkin (Periods 3–7).

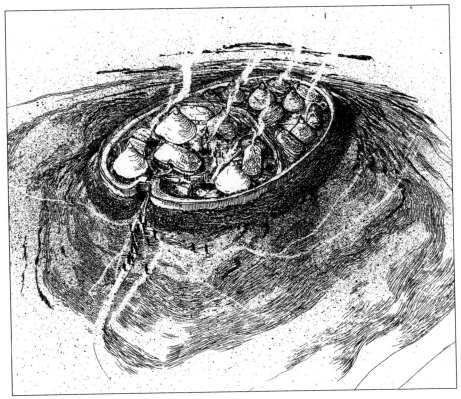

Fig 52 Reconstruction of Dundonald as an Iron Age hillfort (© Crown copyright, reproduced courtesy of Historic Scotland).

PERIODS 2A AND 2B (*c.* 500 BC–*c.* AD 1000)

The character of the Period 2a and 2b buildings and their defences appears to show the transition from a hillfort, with several large round wooden houses, to a *dun* with a drystone rampart and subrectangular buildings (Fig 52). That a single community could sustain continuous occupation at Dundonald is likely. As has been noted by Geoffrey Barrow, it is quite conceivable that by the Roman period 'a single tribe [the *Damnonii*] occupied the easily traversed territory from Kyle to the lower Clyde and even the Lennox, taking in Ayr, Irvine, Glasgow and Dumbarton' (1989, 162).

The absence of precise dating evidence necessitates an interpretation based on broad characteristics and inference. It is noteworthy that the Period 2a roundhouses of Groups I–III all respected the site of Structure 17 (Period 2b); but this is probably due to the fact that the Period 2a buildings exploited all available space on the hill summit. The Period 2b hall either overlay a fourth house site or was located in order to exploit the open area on to which the three earlier house sites had opened.

The nature of the defences enclosing the site prior to the construction of the drystone rampart is uncertain, although a fragment of palisade on the lower terrace to the north of the exposed drystone circuit may imply a wider enclosure of timber construction. Aerial photographic evidence (Fig 5) and fieldwalking suggest that more house sites of similar dimensions to those already revealed may exist around the lower slopes of the hill, suggesting a nucleated and possibly multivallate fortification.

It is postulated that at some point after the 5th century AD, the hillfort was converted to accommodate, on its highest point, a smaller, heavily defended circuit forming a citadel, protecting relatively few structures within (Period 2b). If we assume that the entrance was essentially the same for both the Period 2 layouts, it is likely that Structure 15 formed part of the entrance defences. This interpretation of the evidence reflects three basic indicators: the size and scale of the enclosure, the presence of certain datable artefacts, and the use of timber-laced ramparts.

That the Period 2a fort dates from the late Iron Age is indicated by the range and quality of the finds retrieved. Shale or lignite bracelets (see p. 104, no. 82), glass beads (nos 105–6) and a La Tène B fibula pin (no. 51) are all indicative of settlement during the 4th and 5th centuries AD. The structural evidence comprises groups of roundhouses, which follow a consistent stratigraphic sequence, from houses with earthfast posts to those of ring-ditch and inner post construction. Both types represent houses of about 8.5–9m diameter and are comparable with houses found at Broxmouth, East Lothian (Hill 1979; 1982). The successive building on each of the main house sites indicates an extended period of settlement, but how long this was maintained is not clear. A change in intensity of occupation for the Period 2b fort might be implied by the decline in the range and number of artefacts from occupation horizons. The most diagnostic of these were sherds of 6th to 7th-century 'E Ware' (see pp. 90–2), all of which were found in association with the drystone rampart. However, the spearheads (nos 68 and 69), crucibles (nos 110 and 111) and knife (no. 73) could all be contemporary.

In terms of its plan and layout, Dundonald follows a pattern similar to other fortified sites that were occupied up to the early historic period, such as Dundurn, Dunollie and Dumbarton (Alcock 2003). At these sites, a nucleated fortification was established around a rocky hill summit. The size of the inner enclosure at Dundonald was perhaps only some 1,200 m² and the presence of a few distinctive buildings within it gives an indication of hierarchical use. According to Leslie Alcock's terminology, Dundonald would qualify as a site with a 'dominant rock boss surrounded by terraces' (Alcock et al. 1989, 210). Indeed, Alcock suggests that the form of the defences of Dundurn, Dunollie and Dumbarton was not so much planned, as dictated by the hills upon which they were set. 'The hill was primary, the defences secondary, and the close relationship of hill and defences was something which evolved with time' (Alcock et al. 1989, 210). The nucleated nature of the fortification at Dundonald is further implied by the discovery of vitrified stonework, apparently in situ, to the W of the Period 6 tower-house. This suggests that the distinctive semi-circular earthwork above the 53m contour immediately W of the tower may be part of the Period 2 layout. It appears to have extended the natural terrace along the northern edge of the hill to form a lower enclosure around the 'citadel'.

This impression of a developing site seems entirely reasonable for a traditional site of lordly power. In many ways, the archaeological evidence elucidates the development of Kyle as part of Strathclyde. In this context, Dundonald Castle Hill was a prominent feature, topographically impressive and now shown to have been intensively occupied for many centuries before the early Middle Ages.

The second key feature of the early occupation was the timber-laced rampart, which was subsequently vitrified (although only a short section of it was in fact revealed). Timber-laced rampart construction represents a distinct tradition, extending for several centuries from the 7th or 6th century BC onwards (MacKie 1976). However, although the use of timber in the fabric of the wall was evidently intended to strengthen it, over time it may have had the opposite effect as the timbers rotted away (Ritchie and Ritchie 1991, 91). The subsequent vitrefaction of the rampart also points to the high status of the Period 2b settlement at Dundonald. The setting of the fire and the gradual acceleration of its effect within the wall structure are unlikely to have occurred by accident and would more probably have been the result of deliberate action. Although it is possible that timber buildings close to or against the inner face of the rampart might have amplified the effect (cf. Alcock and Alcock 1992, 260), an experiment carried out at East Tullos led Ian Ralston to conclude that 'there can be little doubt that enclosures which display widespread evidence of altered stonework demonstrate very considerable pyrotechnical abilities on the part of the fire-raisers' (1986, 38). More recent consideration of the phenomenon has encouraged Ralston (2004) to explore whether such destruction may well have been symbolic or even ritualised. It would certainly have been spectacular and visible for miles around.

The importance of Dundonald within the kingdom of Strathclyde in the Early Historic period is also suggested by the presence of E-ware pottery, imported from the Continent. This class of pottery is found widely on many sites in western Britain and Ireland, though the precise mechanisms by which it got there, whether by trade or gift exchange, are at present imperfectly understood. E-ware is generally dated to the 6th–7th century and at the very least suggests the presence of occupants of high status and prestige at the site, enjoying social, political or economic contact with other populations along the western seaboard of Britain and the European mainland (Lane and Campbell 2000, 241–3). A thermoluminescence date for the destruction of the rampart centred around c. AD 1000 places Dundonald within the wider historical context of the political upheavals of Viking Age Strathclyde.

PERIOD 3 (c. 1000–c. 1241)

The reuse of existing prehistoric or Roman defences is a common feature of Norman castles in Britain and Ireland (cf. Talbot 1974, 52). The evidence for the construction of a motte at Dundonald may reasonably be associated with the granting of North Kyle (Kyle Stewart, or Walter's Kyle) to Walter Fitzalan by David I or Malcolm IV in the 1150s or 1160s (RRS, I, 286, no. 310; cf. 39), and with Walter's decision to make Dundonald his *caput*. The large amount of vitrified stonework in the fabric of the 15th-century barmkin walls further demonstrates that much of the Period 2 rampart would have been extant even at that date.

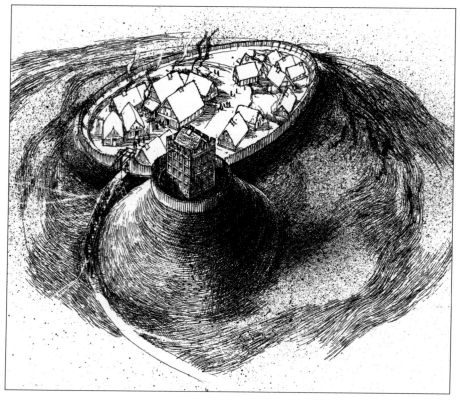

Fig 53 Reconstruction of Dundonald as a Motte and Bailey castle (© Crown copyright, reproduced courtesy of Historic Scotland).

Therefore the addition of a motte-like earthwork to what was probably an extant ringwork in the 12th century would have made good practical and strategic sense (Fig 53).

The siting of the motte at the E end of the Castle Hill was probably intended to help protect the established route on to the site from the east. Although largely obscured by the Period 4 N gatehouse tower, the motte's base is today represented by the 53m contour to the east. Archaeological evidence for this period of occupation was largely obscured by later more massive forms of building. However, late 13th-century pottery found in the backfilling of the redundant post-pits of a fragmentary hall-like structure (Structure 16a) suggests that it should be associated with this phase of occupation.

Although the structural evidence for this period is slight, its significance is enhanced considerably by the consideration that it was at this time that Dundonald came to be closely associated with the early Stewarts. There is a strong likelihood that the granting of Kyle Stewart to Walter I and the establishment of a castle at Dundonald were part of a royal strategy to confront the military and political threats arising from the south and west. It is significant that the site chosen was already most probably a place of acknowledged local significance and a traditional seat of lordly power. This exploitation of an existing local symbol of power may well have played a part in assisting in the imposition of a new system of lordship, with its centralised power base.

There are numerous precedents for the reoccupation of earlier fortifications during the early Middle Ages in Scotland (cf. Creighton 2002, 38–9). The excavations at Crookston, south of Glasgow, also suggest the association of a ringwork and the early followers of the Stewarts (Talbot 1974, 48; Lewis 2003). Neighbouring Carmunnock and Camphill had Norman ringworks, as did the episcopal castle in Glasgow, whose early medieval layout itself appears to have followed the lie of the land, much in the Iron Age tradition (Talbot 1974, 49; Yeoman 1995, 88). The castle of Auldhill, near Portencross (Ayrshire), was found on excavation to have comprised an early medieval hall-house, set within the remains of a multi-phase hillfort, which, again echoing Dundonald, showed signs of both vitrifaction and an inner defensive circuit, into which the 12th-century incoming Ross family had built their hall house (Caldwell *et al.* 1998, 67–8). Similarly, at Dunnideer Castle (Aberdeenshire), an 11th-century earth and timber castle was fashioned within the defences of the vitrified drystone rampart of a hillfort. Sometime in the 13th century a stone tower, albeit with no motte, was built within these defences, which were themselves regularised in stone (Simpson 1935, 463–5).

At Dundonald, the juxtaposition of the likely motte and the relict vitrified rampart would in effect have provided the layout of a motte-and-bailey type of castle. This type of defensive scheme is found elsewhere in Scotland and could also be relatively long-lived. At Castlemilk, Huntly, Edzell and Crookston, for example, such arrangements persisted into the 13th century (Talbot 1974, 55; Macguire 2000, 43; Lewis 2003). Unfortunately, the motte at Dundonald was later levelled to provide a platform for the N gatehouse tower in Period 4. Consequently the details of any structures sited on its summit have been lost, but we may expect them to have comprised at least a tower, of timber or of stone.

Associated with the motte was a hall (Structure 16a), built over the levelled remains of the Period 2b house or hall. The building was defined by a series of earthfast posts, which were identified archaeologically as voids in the platform, suggesting that the platform was built around them. This technique has been noted elsewhere in various contexts where there was insufficient depth of soft material into which post-holes could be dug. Drystone dwarf walls or building platforms serving a similar purpose, for example, have been noted at Finlaggan, on Islay (Argyll), and at Auldill, near Portencross (Ayrshire) (Caldwell *et al.* 1998, 67–8). The walls in these instances acted as little more than stable bases on to which a steeply pitched roof could be securely fixed. This practice may be documented through a series of earth-and-timber and stone-and-timber buildings at Finlaggan, covering a period from the 12th century to the end of the 15th century, and was to continue in the post-medieval longhouses and blackhouses of the western seaboard and Highlands. The survival of the evidence for the hall was due entirely to the fact that the later courtyard buildings were located further to the west. It is highly likely that the other associated timber features identified beside the hall represent ancillary structures. In size, the Dundonald Period 3 hall may be compared with the buildings at Cruggleton (Ewart 1985) and Lismahon, in Ulster

(Waterman 1959, 153–5), both of which were also built as part of the early medieval reoccupation of a prehistoric or early historic fortification.

PERIOD 4 (*c*. 1241–*c*. 1300)

The remains of the gatehouse discovered on the E flank of the Castle Hill marks a major period of rebuilding in stone at Dundonald (Fig 51). Although it had been clear to castle scholars from MacGibbon and Ross (1887–92, I, 167–72, fig 133–40) through to Simpson (1950) and Cruden (1981, 120–2) that much of the surviving form and fabric of the tower-house (Period 6) had been influenced in some way by an earlier stone building, nothing was known about the layout of the stone castle that predated the late 14th-century one until the recent excavations.

It is probable that the conversion of the earth and timber castle of Walter Fitzalan into one of stone began around 1200 and continued through the 13th century. By 1230, in advance of an attack by Norse forces, Rothesay Castle on Bute, another Stewart fortress in the west, had been reconstructed by Alan or Walter Stewart as a circular stone castle of enclosure, probably taking its form from an earlier earthwork (Pringle 1998, 152). Dundonald's defences would doubtless also have been improved around this time, though the only evidence of such is that the Period 3 motte base was reinforced by stone revetment, creating a strengthened apron with a pronounced batter (Fig 18). It is quite likely that parts of the earthwork defences would have been retained while the castle was being progressively rebuilt in stone. The fortifications of castles such as Ludlow, Richmond, Llanstephan, Exeter and Pontesbury, for example, were all upgraded over a prolonged period by the gradual introduction of stone elements into a existing earth and timber layout (King and Alcock 1969, 108).

A major phase of rebuilding in stone probably occurred in the mid to late 13th century. This saw Dundonald transformed into a kite-shaped castle of enceinte, with a twin-towered gatehouse at each acute angle and other towers, whose existence is assumed but has yet to be verified, at the obtuse angles (Fig 54). Our principal evidence for the form of the castle consists of the bases of the two gatehouses, the western one underlying the later Period 6 tower-house and the eastern one partially revealed by excavation. Unfortunately the excavations were unable to trace the line of the curtain walls that would have linked these structures, though it seems likely that they would have followed in some way the break of slope around the 56–7m contour on the south-east, south and west sides of the hill and that around the 53–4m contour on the north. The excavation of a series of test pits in the terrace behind the latter showed a deep accumulation of topsoil, though the edge of the terrace had been softened by the later dumping of rubble and debris from the ruined castle.

The lack of written records for the castle until the end of the 13th century has little bearing on the question of its date, as many castles known from archaeology to have been in existence for more than a century are mentioned for the first time during the Wars of Independence. Our sources are equally mute as to the patron of the new works, raising the question as to whether they are more likely to have been undertaken by the Stewarts or by the English forces of occupation. The burden of evidence so far assembled, however, suggests that the rebuilding of Dundonald

Fig 54 Reconstruction of Dundonald as a Castle of Enclosure with two twin-towered gatehouses (© Crown copyright, reproduced courtesy of Historic Scotland).

was carried out by one of the Stewarts before the Wars of Independence began, though whether or not it was complete before the castle was slighted in Phase 5 cannot be known for certain, since only the foundations and lower parts of the walls survive.

Twin-towered gatehouses with a defended gate-passage set between a pair of rounded or D-shaped towers developed in the Île de France in the early years of the 13th century. Doubtless they were inspired by the gates of late Roman forts and town walls; but during the course of the 13th century they acquired some particular characteristics, notably the provision of portcullises, murder holes, embrasures and often an outer draw-bridge to protect the wooden gate itself. They could also stand up to three storeys high. Among the earliest examples are those found in the fortresses built in the reign of Philip II Augustus (1180–1223), such as the Louvre (Paris) and Dourdan (Châtelain 1988, 178–9, 219; Fleury and Kruta 2000, 48–59; Gardelles 1986, 87; Salch 1979, 425–6; 1987, 96–8). Similar gates dating from the time of his grand-son, Louis IX (1226–70), include Angers (c.1230) and Boulogne-sur-Mer (Mesqui 2001, 18–19; Salch 1979, 40–2, 182–4).

Twin-towered gatehouses also became common features of the major royal and baronial castles built in England, Scotland, Wales and Ireland in the course of the 13th century, and were also imitated on a smaller scale in some others. One of the earliest known examples in England is King John's northern gate at Dover, which the French attacked and partially destroyed in 1216 (King 1988, 117; Goodall 2000). Other early examples from the 1220s include Kenilworth, Montgomery, Beeston and Bolingbroke (Brown 1976, 98–9; King 1988, 117–21; Kenyon 1990, 65–70; McNeill 1992, 98–101). The fashion was quickly taken up in Ireland, with Lady Rohesia de Verdon's Castle Roche (c. 1225–35) and Hugh II de Lacy's Carrickfergus (1226–42) being among the earliest examples (McNeill 1997, 85–100).

There is some variation in the design of these twin-towered gates. In some, like William Marshal's outer gate at Chepstow, built from 1189 onwards, the towers were initially virtually independent of one another, with communication between them only possible at the wallhead (Turner 2002, 45, 53). At Tonbridge (Fig 55), however, the towers of the gatehouse built by Gilbert de Clare, earl of Hertford, in the late 1260s, formed part of a unified residential block, containing chambers flanking the upper part of the gate-passage on the first floor and a great hall oversailing it on the second (Oliphant 1992, 14–15; cf. Toy 1954, 243–4). This design (Fig 56) was repeated in the E gate of de Clare's massive castle of Caerphilly, Glamorgan, begun in 1268 and completed by 1272 (Johns 1978; RCAHMW 2000, 51–104). Although some have argued that such gatehouses, or 'keep-gatehouses', combined the functions of keep and gatehouse and would have been independently defensible against the rest of the castle, in most cases their defensibility from within was no more than one would normally expect of any mural tower. It is clear, however, that they often represented a residential unit of considerable standing, which in many cases would probably have accommodated the keeper of the castle and his household.

In terms of size, the widths and depths of such gatehouses (or *châtelets*, as they are known in French) ranged from 27.5m and 24.5m respectively at Beaumaris (Anglesey, 1295–1330) (Brown, Colvin and Taylor 1963, I, 395–408; Taylor 1980, 24–6), to 29m and 19m at Aberystwyth (1277–89) (Brown, Colvin and Taylor 1963, I, 299–308; Spurgeon 1975; Kenyon 1990, 74, fig 3.8), 25.5m and 17.5m at Arsuf in Palestine (c. 1240–60) (Roll and Tal 1999, 1–62; Roll et al. 2000), and 23m and 17.5m at Roscommon, in Ireland (1269–85) (Leask 1946, 67–9; McNeill 1997, 96–100). Also in Ireland, a smaller group ranging in width between 14m and 17m and in depth between 10m and 13m includes Ballylahan, Lea, Ballintubber, Dungarvan and Kiltartan (McNeill 1997, figs 56, 73). In most such cases, the depth required for the accommodation inside the gatehouse led to them being set astride the curtain wall, usually with no more than half projecting forward from it. The gate-passage would be flanked at ground level by relatively narrow elongated D-shaped guard chambers, sometimes, though not always, subdivided.

At Dundonald, however, the evidence from the W gate – and to some extent also the E gate – suggests a slightly different form. First, the towers were more than semi-circular externally (Fig 57). Second, if we are correct in assuming that the E wall of the Period 6 tower-house stands directly on the foundation of the back wall of the 13th-century W gatehouse, it would appear likely that the latter stood almost entirely forward of the curtain wall. The excavated evidence suggests that this was also the case with the E gatehouse. In both these respects and also in

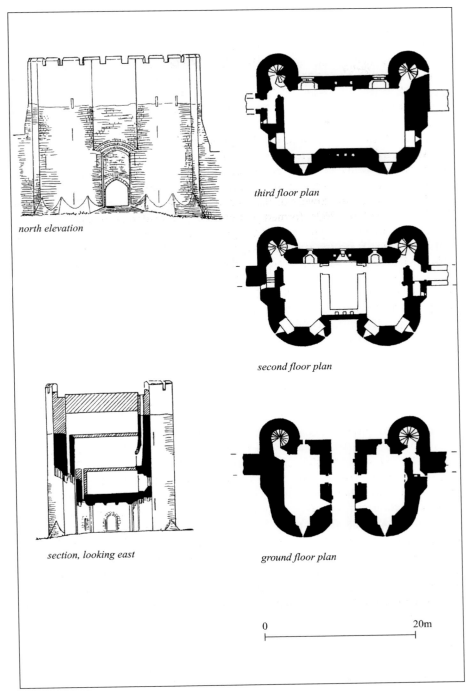

north elevation

third floor plan

second floor plan

section, looking east

ground floor plan

0   20m

Fig 55 Tonbridge Castle: plans, elevation and section of the gatehouse (after Toy 1954).

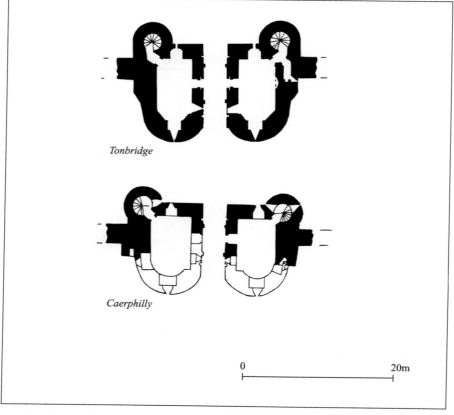

Tonbridge

Caerphilly

0   20m

Fig 56 Plans of the castle gatehouses at Tonbridge (after Toy 1954) and Caerphilly (after RCAHMW 2000).

terms of its size, Dundonald finds closer parallels with another group of 13th-century gatehouses.

At Carrickfergus, Antrim (Fig 58), the gatehouse is thrust forward at the end of a rock outcrop, forming part of a new outer ward added to the castle by Hugh II de Lacy in 1226–42. The towers are more than semi-circular, and are not backed by any additional chambers within the castle enceinte (McNeill 1981, 44–5, figs 3–4, 16–17; 1997, 88, fig 50). The rather similar gatehouse at Nenagh (Tipperaray) may be contemporary, if not slightly earlier, though here there does seem to have been some form of extension on the inside (McNeill 1997, 28, 50–2, 93–4, figs 16, 50, 53).

At Harlech (Fig 58), the castle built in North Wales for Edward I between 1283 and 1290, under the superintendence of Master James of St George, the rounded towers of the gatehouse are also more than semi-circular, but are backed by an accommodation block with rounded stair turrets at the corners (Brown, Colvin and Taylor 1963, 357–65; Taylor 1988). The similarity of Harlech's gatehouse to that at Kildrummy (Aberdeenshire) was observed by W. Douglas

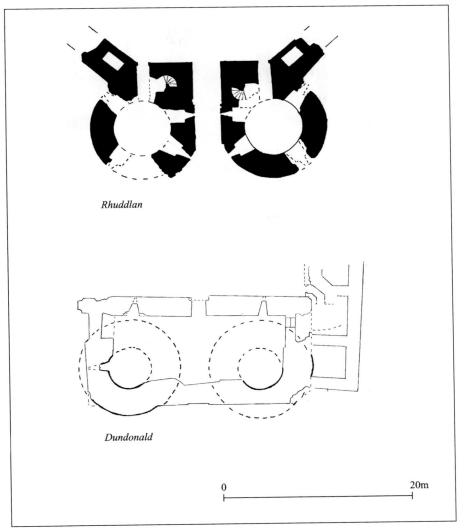

Rhuddlan

Dundonald

0   20m

Fig 57 Comparison between the W gatehouse at Dundonald Castle and the
N gate at Rhuddlan Castle (after Taylor 1972).

Simpson, who noted that not only did Edward himself visit the castle in August 1296 and October 1303 and his son, Edward of Caernavon, take it in September 1306, but that James of St George was also in Scotland between 1298 and 1305 (1965, 4–5, 9). Here the gatehouse is also astride the wall, the D-shaped rooms within the rounded towers being backed on the ground floor (which is all that survives) by rectangular chambers, one of them containing a fireplace. It is clear, however, that the gatehouse at Kildrummy was not built in isolation but was part of a building operation that also saw the construction of the two adjacent curtains and the adjacent towers (Fig 60). These and other works seem to have been part of

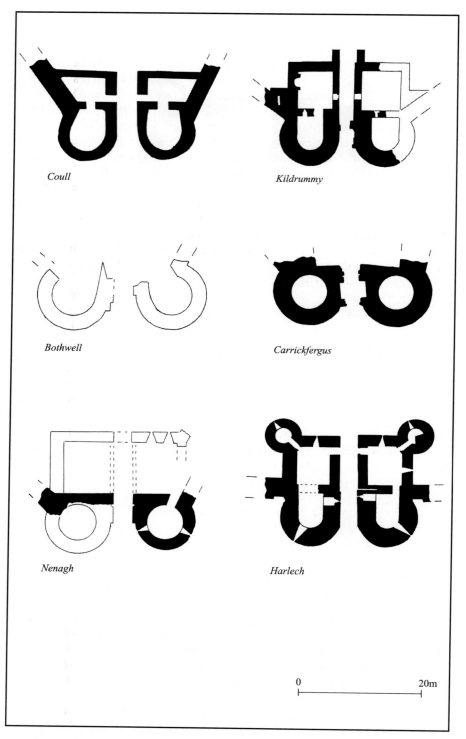

Fig 58 Plans of the castle gatehouses at Coull (after Simpson 1924), Kildrummy (after Simpson 1965), Bothwell (after Simpson 1978), Carrickfergus (after McNeill 1981), Nenagh (after McNeill 1997) and Harlech (after Taylor 1988).

a general reconstruction of the older stone castle of the earls of Mar carried out by the English. As Stewart Cruden has observed, the similarities with Harlech and the parallels of the fireplaces with those at Conway (1283–89) suggest that this occurred in the 1290s (1981, 74–8; cf. Apted 1963; Tabraham 1986). The possible role of Master James has in any case been overstated, since there is little evidence to suggest that he was himself a designer of castles (Coldstream 2003).

Another Scottish castle that appears to have been rebuilt under the English occupation was Coull, also in Aberdeenshire. This was excavated by A. Marshall Mackenzie from 1912 onwards and by W. Douglas Simpson in 1923. The original castle, built by the Durwards in the 1230s, was in the hands of Duncan, earl of Fife, when he was assassinated in September 1286. In 1299, his widow, Isabella, conveyed Coull and Lumphanan to Sir John Hastings, lord of Abergavenny, in return for a payment of £80 each year, to offset her losses caused by the war and the depredations of Sir Herbert de Morham (CDS, II, no. 1108). Although she was reinfiefed with her English lands in March 1302, she did not immediately receive back her Scottish ones (CDS, II, no. 1299), which effectively remained in the hands of the English king. In July 1305, when John of Strathbogie, earl of Athole and Edward's warden and justiciary north of Forth, was ordered to return Coull to the countess of Fife, he reported having spent £540 in repairing the castles of Coull and Aberdeen and garrisoning them with 20 men-at-arms and 40 sergeants-on-foot (CDS, II, no. 1682; Simpson 1924, 47–51). Although the gatehouse excavated by Simpson was very poorly preserved, enough was left to indicate that, like Kildrummy, it was flanked by rounded towers with guard chambers behind them; it also had a drawbridge pit in front, containing the burnt remains of a timber bridge (Simpson 1924, 60, 70–2, figs 4, 13, 20). Its construction seems likely to have been contemporary with Kildrummy's, probably between 1296 and 1305.

Not all Scottish twin-towered gatehouses, however, can be attributed to Edward I and his engineers. Bothwell Castle (Figs 58, 60) was twice taken by the English in 1296 and 1301 and twice dismantled by the Scots in 1314 and 1337. The gatehouse, however, with rounded towers and a drawbridge pit like Kildrummy and Coull seems to have been under construction and incomplete before the castle first surrendered to Edward. It was left outside the castle when it was finally rebuilt in the later 14th century. Its foundations and those of the adjoining unfinished curtains appear to have been laid out either by Walter of Moray, who acquired Bothwell in 1242 and was occupying the castle by 1278, or by his son, William 'the Rich', who lost it in 1296 (Simpson 1978, 2–13; Tabraham 1994, 2–9). This dating is mirrored by that of a number of smaller gatehouses of similar design (Fig 59), including Montgomery (c. 1224–35) (Lloyd and Knight 1973; Kenyon 1990, 65, fig 3.4), White Castle (Monmouth, 1267–?) (Knight 2000, 1241–3), Criccieth (Caernavonshire, 1230–40) (Avent 1989, 11–13; Kenyon 1990, 69; contra Johns 1970), Caerlaverock (Dumfries, 1270s) (O'Neil 1982), and Castell Bryn Amlwg (Salop, ?1267–76) (Kenyon 1990, 68–9, fig 3.6).

Perhaps the closest parallel to the gates at Dundonald, however, are those at Rhuddlan which also stand at opposing angles of a lozenge-shaped *enceinte* (Figs 57 and 60). The dimensions of these two gates are virtually identical to those of the W gate at Dundonald. Rhuddlan was built for Edward I between 1277 and

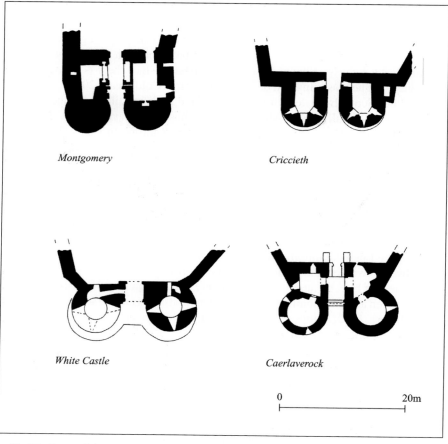

Fig 59 Plans of the castle gatehouses at Montgomery (after Lloyd and Knight 1973),
Criccieth (after Johns 1970), White Castle (after Knight 2000) and Caerlaverock
(after O'Neil 1982).

1282 (Brown, Colvin and Taylor 1963, I, 318–72; Taylor 1972). Edward's castle
at Aberystwyth also dates from this period (1277–89); and, although its gatehouse
is larger, the castle itself also has a kite-shaped plan (Fig 60) (Brown, Colvin and
Taylor 1963, I, 299–308; Spurgeon 1975; Kenyon 1990, 74, fig 3.8).

This brief survey of comparative castle and gatehouse designs leads us
to conclude that the likeliest time for the laying out of Dundonald's stone walls
and gatehouses would have been in the second half of the 13th century, most
probably in the 1270s–80s. Like Bothwell, it appears to have predated the English
occupation during the Wars of Independence, though – also like Bothwell – it is
uncertain how far construction had progressed before the castle fell to the English.
Although the ground floors of the gatehouses had evidently been built, it is not
known whether they stood complete to the wallhead nor whether the curtain walls
and their flanking towers had yet been finished. The apparent lack of structures in

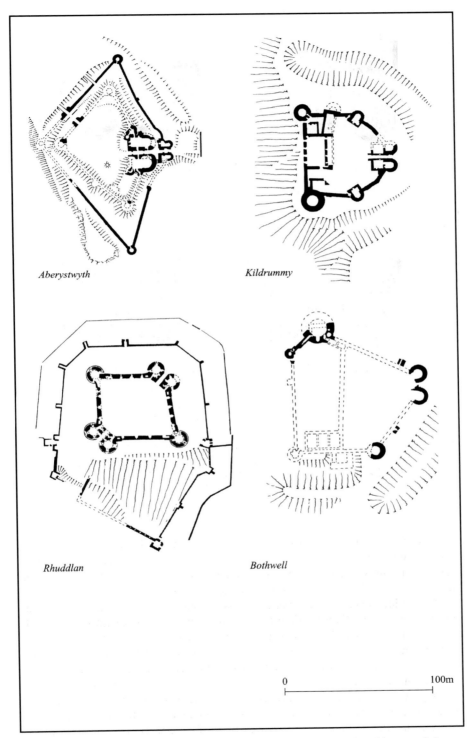

Fig 60 Plans of the castles of Aberystwyth (after Spurgeon [1975]), Kildrummy (after Simpson 1965), Rhuddlan (after Taylor 1972) and Bothwell (after Simpson 1978).

the central area of the castle might indeed suggest that building was incomplete or only just finished when the castle was destroyed in Period 5.

Identifying the Patron of the Thirteenth-century Castle

The likeliest person to associate with the transformation of Dundonald into an up-to-date castle of its time is Alexander Stewart of Dundonald, who was fourth Stewart of Scotland from 1241 until his death in 1283. Alexander Stewart was certainly as wealthy and as powerful as Walter of Murray (de Moravia), the possible builder of Bothwell Castle (Simpson 1978, 2; Tabraham 1994, 2), and the earls of Mar, who built the early stone castle of Kildrummy (Simpson 1965, 4; Tabraham 1986). When on pilgrimage to Compostela between 1253 and 1255, Alexander may also have visited Coucy, north-east of Paris, the home of Mary de Coucy, second wife of King Alexander II. It is generally recognised that the now destroyed donjon at Coucy le Château, built by Enguerrard III of Coucy between 1225 and 1245, may have been the inspiration for similar, albeit smaller, towers at Bothwell and possibly Kildrummy (Tabraham 1990, 36–8; 1997, 40; Yeoman 1995, 99); and by the same token the twin-towered Porte de Soissons, which from c. 1220 onwards gave access to the adjacent walled town of Coucy (Salch 1979, 372–4), could, like other similar contemporary French examples, have influenced Bothwell's unfinished gatehouse. Alexander Stewart's direct acquaintance with the new castles of the Île de France may well have influenced his work at Dundonald.

After 1260, Alexander III was obliged to prepare for the full-scale invasion of the west coast of Scotland by Håkon IV of Norway. Alexander Stewart was almost certainly involved in these preparations. Some direct evidence for this exists in the form of a document dated 9 September 1261 relating to a loan. This relates that Alexander Stewart acknowledged a debt of £200 to Deulecreusse, son of Aaron the Jew, and undertook to repay it on 8 July 1262. If he failed to do so, he would have to pay 2d. per week in interest for every pound that remained unpaid, while pledging his lands, rents and goods for the recovery of the whole debt and any interest (CDS, V, 137, no. 21). It is hard not to see this loan as part of the preparations for the Norse attack, including the funding of new works at Dundonald, the main Stewart stronghold in Kyle. How much building work £200 would pay for at this time is hard to say. In 1302, Edward I spent sums of around £900 and £1,370 respectively in fortifying the royal manor of Linlithgow and the motte-and-bailey castle of Selkirk with timber walls and towers, stone-and-timber gatehouses, and outer ditches (Brown, Colvin and Taylor 1963, I, 412–15). The two Welsh castles that bear the closest similarity to Dundonald, however, Rhuddlan (1277–9) and Aberystwyth (1277–89), cost Edward at least £4,800 and £4,300 respectively (Brown, Colvin and Taylor 1963, I, 299–307, 320–1). On this basis, £200 might perhaps have gone some way towards the cost of building one of the gatehouses at Dundonald, but nothing more. Alexander Stewart, however, would have had access to considerable resources of his own in addition to the loan, which may not in any case have been unique. A measure of his resources may be indicated by his confidence in his ability to repay the debt in one year, presumably from his own rents.

Elsewhere at this time Walter Stewart, earl of Menteith, was engaged in Argyll fighting the MacSweens in Knapdale and Arran, while the king himself was strengthening the defences of the castle of Dumbarton. The whole episode culminated in the Battle of Largs in 1263, when the Scots prevailed against the Norse, with Alexander Stewart playing a significant part as commander of the Scottish army (Duncan 1975, 577–80; Anderson 1922 II, 607–34).

The presence of a well in the southern tower of the E gatehouse, along with the rock-cut cistern in the courtyard, might well be an indication of lessons learnt at the siege of Rothesay Castle by the Norse in 1230. Although the excavation cleared only the upper 1.85m of infill from the well, in order to reach the water table it is estimated that its depth must have been around 30m. In the 13th-century hilltop castles of Beeston (Cheshire) and Montgomery the wells are 112m and 63m deep respectively, while at Criccieth (Caernarvonshire), Sanquhar (Dumfriesshire) and Brampton Bryan (Herefordshire) the well is also located in a gatehouse. The significance of this aspect of the Period 4 castle is that Dundonald was sufficiently important to warrant the cutting of a deep well, the location of which was determined by the strategic requirements of the defenders. The water supply also appears to have been supplemented by a rainwater cistern (Ruckley 1990).

The rectangular stone building (Structure 21) that later defined the N side of the Period 6 inner courtyard apparently predated the barmkin walls and may also therefore date from Period 4. Its location, orientation and longevity raise the possibility that it was the chapel of St Ninian, whose chaplain's stipend is mentioned in 1434 as having been established in antiquity (ER, IV, 596). The same entry in the Exchequer account, however, describes this chapel as being near the castle (*prope castrum de Dundonalde*), rather than in it or next to it (*in, juxta*). The relationship between the castle and the chapel would therefore appear to have been more like that between Rothesay Castle and the related chapel of St Bride, which was located some distance outside its walls (Pringle 1998, 155, 158).

PERIOD 5 (*c.* 1300–*c.* 1371)

The excavated evidence suggests that, whether or not it had ever been completed, the E gatehouse was subsequently destroyed above its foundations and lower masonry courses. It was then rebuilt in timber and daub above its masonry base, before being destroyed once again, this time by fire. After that it was abandoned. As nothing survives of the W gatehouse above 4–5m in height, it is very possible that its structural history was the same as the E gatehouse's, though it has not yet been possible to confirm this by excavation. Although the dating of these events is imprecise and direct documentary evidence is lacking, it is likely that they occurred sometime between 1286 and 1305.

The period following the Battle of Falkirk (1298) is likely to have been a critical one in the history of Dundonald. After the Scottish defeat on 22 July, Edward I pressed on to Ayr where he found that the castle had been burnt down on the orders of Robert Bruce (Innes 1832, 328; Barrow 1976, 145–6; Watson 1998, 68). Considering its proximity to Ayr and its potential for use as a garrison point by English forces, it is likely that Dundonald would have suffered the same fate.

Nevertheless, Edward succeeded in recapturing intact most of the Lowland castles including Edinburgh, Stirling, Lochmaben and Jedburgh; and, from 1298 until c. 1301, many of the castles in English hands were rebuilt and strengthened. Although there is no documentary evidence for anything similar occurring at Dundonald, the excavated evidence from the E gatehouse suggests that after its initial destruction it too was rebuilt, though in timber. The silence of the sources concerning Dundonald may be due to Edward's grant of James Stewart's lands to Henry de Lacy, earl of Lincoln. As at Bothwell, which was granted to Aymer de Valence, the costs of any building or repair work there would then have been borne by de Lacy and would not have been entered in the royal accounts. It is therefore perfectly possible that Dundonald, like a number of other castles, benefited from the general programme of rebuilding and consolidation that was carried out by the English. Dumfries, Edinburgh and Hermitage were all repaired at this time, while at Lochmaben Sir Robert de Clifford built a 'peel' on the lochside c.1km from the slighted castle of the Bruces. In August 1299 this new castle was successfully defended against the earl of Carrick. Similar 'peels' with wooden towers, gates and ditches were constructed at Linlithgow, Selkirk and Kirkintilloch (Brown, Colvin and Taylor 1963, I, 409–20; cf. Watson 1998, 67–94).

When John de Soules became guardian of Scotland early in 1301, pressure increased on the English forces in the south-west (Barrow 1976, 161, 170–2). A letter sent from Renfrew to Edward I by John Marshall, the earl of Lincoln's baillie or steward of the former Stewart lands, towards the end of 1301, describes the advance of John de Soules from Galloway into Cunningham with 300 men and asks for immediate assistance (CDS, II, 286, no. 1121; Barrow and Royan 1985, 179; Watson 1998, 138). This implies that at that time Dundonald would no longer have had an English garrison. After that date, de Lacy turned his attention to Inverkip, further north, near the lower Clyde, in order to hold it against an expected Scottish attack. The mass of burnt wood, daub and nails revealed in the excavation over and around the E gatehouse at Dundonald may well represent the destruction of de Lacy's wooden 'peel' by de Soules on his way north, or by the Scots following the temporary truce made in January 1302. As at Ayr and at Selkirk, where the castle was captured and destroyed by the Scots in 1303, the intention of such an act would have been to deny the English further use of the castle.

Although James, the 5th Stewart, finally submitted to the King Edward I and was granted the return of his forfeited lands in 1306, he died in 1309 and was succeeded by his young son, Walter, still in his minority. There is little likelihood therefore that the period immediately before his death would have seen any major rebuilding at Dundonald; and it is similarly unlikely that Walter III Stewart, who died young in 1327, undertook any significant works there. Walter's wife, however, was Marjorie, the daughter of King Robert Bruce; and although she died from a fall from her horse in March 1316, she bore Walter a son, also named Robert. Robert Stewart's position as heir presumptive to the throne was blocked in 1324 by the birth of a royal prince, who succeeded his father as David II in 1329. It was not until 1371 that Robert Stewart finally ascended the throne as Robert II, the first of a line of Stewart kings to rule over Scotland, and later over England and Ireland as well.

Fig 61 Reconstruction of Dundonald as a tower-house castle (© Crown copyright reproduced courtesy of Historic Scotland).

Period 6 (*c*. 1371–*c*. 1449/50)

With Robert Stewart's accession to the throne in 1371, Dundonald acquired the status of a royal castle. Its present layout (Figs 51 and 61), with a great tower-house dominating a small courtyard and a larger rectangular barmkin, is almost certainly due to Robert II; and it was at Dundonald that he died in 1390. Robert's evident attachment to Dundonald, however, raises the possibility that building work may already havse been in progress before his accession, during the period when his son, John Stewart, was lord of Dundonald. The castle was clearly already inhabitable from the first year of his reign, when he issued charters from it. The lack of references to building works in the Exchequer accounts for his reign is also suggestive, though not conclusive, as such works might have been paid for from other sources, as indeed seems to have been the case at Rothesay (Pringle 1998, 154).

Although the precise date at which the rebuilding of the castle began is therefore open to question, the architectural evidence of the tower-house is consistent with a time of construction towards the end of the 14th century. The use of pointed barrel-vaulting inside the tower-house is a feature that became increasingly common in such buildings from the late 14th century onwards. The application of ribs serving no structural function to the soffit of the vault in the upper hall also finds parallels in the ribbed barrel-vaulting over the three western choir bays of St Giles' kirk in Edinburgh (1385–1419) and in the more elaborate treatment of the same idea, in this case imitating tierceron vaulting, covering the presbytery at Melrose Abbey (Fawcett 1994, 5–7, 33–5; 2002, 230–4). A somewhat later example, with moulded consoles very like those at Dundonald, is the vault over St Mirin's aisle in Paisley Abbey (c. 1499) (Fawcett 2002, 235–7). The robbing of freestone from the tower-house deprives us of information on other architectural details such as mouldings and tracery that might make further comparisons possible, though what remains of the windows in the lower hall is at least consistent with a late 14th-century date.

The remarkable series of armorial bearings that are built into the N and W walls of the tower-house (Figs 32–4), however, point to a date of completion in the reign of Robert II. None the less, some care must be taken in interpreting these carved stones, as they cannot all necessarily be assumed to be contemporary with the building of the tower-house. While there can be little doubt that the prominent lion rampant within the royal tressure, centrally placed on the W wall, and another to the left of it both relate to the king, such emblems displayed on castle walls often denote no more than the builder's acknowledgement that it was from the king that he held his feu. They do not necessarily imply direct royal ownership or residence, and could in theory therefore date from before Robert II's accession. It is also clear that some of the other carved stones have been recycled from elsewhere. The most obvious of these are the fragments of moulding, placed above some of the shields in a crude manner. The two lions opposed, passant gardant are equally unlikely in their present setting at the SW corner of the tower-house, as no attempt has been made to harmonise them with the other carved elements. More significant for dating, however, are the panels relating to the earldoms of Carrick and – if W. D. Simpson was correct – Fife. Simpson proposed associating the latter with the marriage of Robert II's son, Walter, to Isabella, countess of Fife, in 1365; but by 1373 she was dead (RMS, I, 161, no. 443), and by 1377 Walter had married Margaret, daughter of David Barclay of Brechin (RMS, I, nos 652, 689). It seems much more probable, as John Dunbar has suggested, that these two armorials refer respectively to Robert II's first son, John, who was earl of Carrick from 1368 (cf. RMS, I, no. 354), and his third son, Robert, earl of Menteith, who became earl of Fife in 1371 (RMS, I, nos 398, 400, 402, 423; Dunbar 1999, 96, 106 n.11). Both sons appear regularly as witnesses to their father's charters and were often in attendance at court. On this evidence, the arrangement of the five main panels on the west front of the tower-house would have been made after 1371 and have represented the king, Robert II, flanked by armorials referring on the left to his royal and Stewart forebears and on the right to his first two sons, John (the future Robert III) and Robert (the future duke of Albany). As Cruden has remarked, this display of architectural heraldry, while exceptional for its period in a secular context, is contemporary with the earliest surviving collection of Scottish coats of arms, contained in the *Armorial de Gelre* (1370–88), now in the Royal Library in Brussels (1981, 131).

If the heraldry displayed on the outside of the tower serves to associate its construction more firmly with Robert II, it may also point to the identification of the knight and lady represented on the corbels of the W window lighting the high table in the lower hall as King Robert II and second wife and queen, Euphemia, countess of Ross.

In terms of its planning the tower-house at Dundonald may best be understood as an experimental design, which evolved during construction (Figs 29–31). The builders who first conceived it appear to have intended to construct a tower-gatehouse over the ruins of the dismantled twin-towered gatehouse of Alexander Stewart. Its function as a gatehouse would have been at best secondary, since it was in the wrong place to form the main entrance into the castle and was facing in the wrong direction to create much of an impression on anyone approaching it. The gate and pend leading through its basement would also have been too narrow to have formed a major entrance; and, although they could have been – and quite possibly were – made more defensible by the provision of such features as projecting machicolations at the wall-head, murder holes over the pend, and a strong iron yett before the outer gate, the tower can never have been a serious work of fortification. Its appearance as a gate-tower, enhanced by the armorial display on the outer face, was therefore probably always intended to be more symbolic than functional.

The internal planning of the tower was also original. Although the pend running through its centre seems to have been vaulted, the basement areas to north and south of it were covered by timber floors carried on joists. Above the basement was a first-floor hall, enclosed by a plain massive barrel-vault, and above that a second hall, enclosed by a more elaborate barrel-vault with applied ribs. The lower hall, entered directly from inside the castle up an external staircase at the N end of its E wall, would most likely have been intended as a more public space, while the upper hall, reached up a turnpike stair from the upper end of the lower hall, would have been reserved for the more private use of the king and his courtiers.

The lower hall had all the features that one would normally expect of one. The main door at the northern end opened into a screens passage and service, above which was a timber gallery. The service also communicated with the basement cellar by a mural stair in the NE corner. The lack of fireplaces in the lower hall suggests that there would have been a separate kitchen, though some form of heating using braziers would also have been practicable in the central part of the hall where the floor was stone, the smoke escaping through vents in the sides of the vault.

In the upper hall, the orientation was reversed, with the service towards the south and the high table to the north. A curious feature of the domestic arrangements, however, is the apparent lack of any private chamber for the king. In a later period, probably in the 16th century, this problem was evidently overcome by dividing the upper hall into an outer and inner chamber; but there is no evidence to suggest that such an arrangement was ever intended or put into practice in the 14th century. The location of the fireplace roughly in the centre of the west wall, the placing of an oriel window to the east of the high table and a latrine closet in the wall behind it all indicate that the hall was meant to function as a unitary space, the only screen being that enclosing the service at the S end. It is possible that this lack of private space in the building simply reflected Robert II's somewhat ascetic approach to life. It may also be that the timber loft that would have capped the tower would have contained chambers, albeit of a perhaps rather spartan nature. The lack of chambers, however, seems to have been identified as a difficulty at an early stage; for building work was soon put in hand to rectify the problem.

The five-storey chamber block built against the S wall of the tower is clearly secondary to it. It is equally clear that it was not planned when the tower was first built, for its construction resulted in the windows in the S wall of the tower being blocked and the slop drain in the vestibule to the upper hall being made unusable. In its upper levels the annexe contained three floors, each comprising a single chamber, entered apparently from the turnpike stair. The two floors below them, at ground- and first-floor level respectively, were vaulted and each divided into two rooms. The eastern room on the first floor was entered from the east off an external stone staircase; and a slapping in the tower's S wall allowed access to be gained from it to the bottom of the turnpike stair and to the upper end of the lower hall. This room appears to have functioned as a porter's lodge; for next to it another barrel-vaulted room, entered through a small doorway, which could be bolted shut from the outside, and containing a fireplace and latrine, may be identified as a prison. A trap door in its floor also gave sole access to a pit prison, occupying the western half of the basement. No doubt, whether a prisoner was incarcerated in the upper or lower prison would have depended on their status and the perceived danger of their escaping.

The building of the annexe with its separate entrance and porter's lodge might be interpreted as signalling a reorientation of the lower hall. But that does not seem to have been the case. As far as it is possible to tell, the main entrance into the lower hall remained the door at its N end. The porter would have controlled access to the chambers and the upper hall; and he would have warded prisoners awaiting justice in either the lower or upper hall. The separate entrance into the tower through his lodge could also have allowed the king and those of his immediate household to come and go without having to pass through the lower hall.

Robert II's tower-house represents an early example of a type of castle building that was to become ubiquitous in Scotland in later centuries. Although tower-keeps were common in England from the later 11th century, the practice of combining hall and chambers within a single tower was rare in Scotland before the Wars of Independence. Buildings such as Cubbie Roo's castle on Wyre (mid 12th century) and Dunnideer and Yester Castles (mid 13th century) were therefore exceptional for their periods (Cruden 1981, 103–4). In the 14th century, however, tower-houses became increasingly common, with the royal household playing a leading part in their development. One of the earliest was the residential tower that David II began at Edinburgh Castle in 1367 and Robert II completed in 1379 (Fig 62). David's Tower, although largely destroyed in 1573, had an L-plan and formed an important element of the castle's outer defences. The king's hall and private lodging occupied two floors above a vaulted storage basement, while two more floors above them seem to have contained a similar lodging for the queen (MacIvor 1993, 37, fig 19; Cruden 1981, 114; Driscoll and Yeoman 1997, 233–4, figs 72, 156). Robert II also seems to have been responsible for the now-destroyed tower-house, whose foundations, some 15m square, survive at Clunie Castle (Perthshire). From 1377 onwards the king made several payments to the keeper, John Ross, towards the building work there (Dunbar 1999, 95–6). Robert's son,

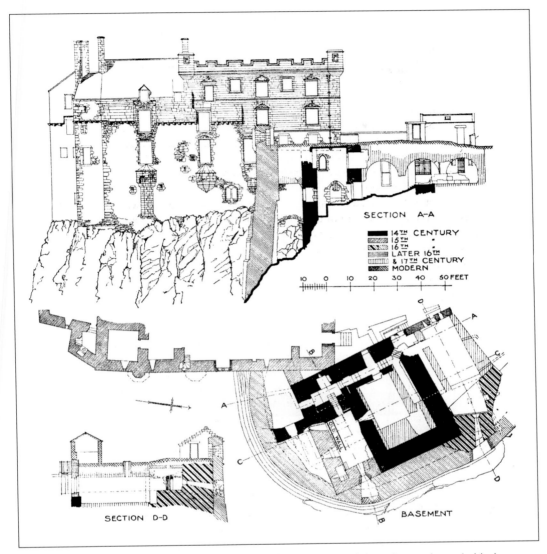

SECTION A-A

■ 14TH CENTURY
▨ 15TH "
▧ 16TH
▤ LATER 16TH
▥ & 17TH CENTURY
▨ MODERN

10 0 10 20 30 40 50 FEET

SECTION D-D

BASEMENT

Fig 62 Edinburgh Castle, David's Tower: plan and section of tower house shown in black
(© Crown copyright, reproduced courtesy of RCAHMS).

Robert III, also appears to have been responsible for a massive tower-house at
Kindrochit (Aberdeenshire). Although Robert II had frequently stayed in the
castle during hunting expeditions, the excavations by W. Douglas Simpson in
1925–6 suggest that in the 1370s and 1380s the castle consisted of an oblong hall-
house with quadrangular corner turrets; inside was a first-floor hall, measuring
30.5 by 9.1m. Subsequently a tower-house, 13.1 by 6.7m internally, was built
over part of the hall-house, the remainder of whose interior space seems to have
become a small unroofed courtyard (Dunbar 1999, 95).

A closer architectural parallel for Robert II's tower-house at Dundonald may
be found in the roughly contemporary tower-house at Carrick Castle (Argyll),

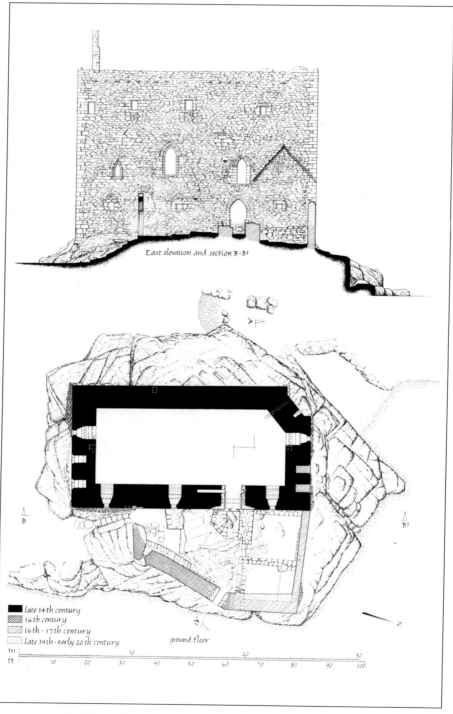

Fig 63 Carrick Castle: plan and E elevation (© Crown copyright, reproduced courtesy of RCAHMS).

which stands on an outcrop of rock jutting into the waters of Loch Goil (Fig 63). Here excavations between 1992 and 1996 revealed remains of an earlier timber and masonry hall, similar to that at Dundonald (Period 3), underlying the later tower-house (Ewart and Baker 1998, 942, 999, figs 4, 27). This site may also have been in Stewart hands before it was granted by Mary, countess of Menteith, to Archibald Campbell of Loch Awe, sometime before 1363 (RRS, VI, 336–7, no. 304); and when the Stewarts took the throne in 1371, the Campbells remained their firm allies in the west (Ewart and Baker 1998, 999–1001). The tower-house was probably built in the last decades of the 14th century. It consists of a rectangular structure, measuring externally 21.1m north–south by 11.3m east–west, with walls 2.2m thick. As at Dundonald, one corner is bevelled, in order to accommodate it to its rocky site. A ground-floor basement divided into three compartments appears to have been covered from the start by a joisted timber floor, though the surviving seating for a barrel-vault suggests that the original intention may have been to vault it. The principal room, however, was a hall at first-floor level, entered through a now-blocked door (1.65m wide) approached by a timber stair or bridge towards the northern end of the west or landward side of the tower; a secondary door facing it in the E wall gave access from within a small barmkin area. As with the lower hall at Dundonald, there is no obvious evidence for a fireplace in the hall; and, although MacGibbon and Ross suggested a possible position for one in the west wall, they noted that it would have been a later insertion, since its flue appears to have run through a window recess on the floor above (1887–92, III, 191). The hall's windows are broadly similar to those of the lower hall at Dundonald; and from either side of the recess of the central of the three windows in the E wall, two sets of mural stairs lead up in opposite directions to the second floor. This was also of timber, and slots in the walls indicate that it wall divided into three chambers. Those at the two extremities were each entered from one of the mural stairs, and both has access to latrine closets. Although the northern chamber had a fireplace inserted into it in a later period, in the 14th century none of these rooms was heated. The central chamber would doubtless have been entered from either or both of the outer ones; its eastern window recess was provided with a *piscina*, allowing it to be identified as an oratory. One of the mural stairs also continued up to the wallhead, whence access may also have been had to a garret within the roof space (RCAHMS 1992, 226–37; Ewart and Baker 1998; MacGibbon and Ross 1887–92, III, 186–92).

The tower-house erected by Archibald (the 'Grim') Douglas at Threave (Kirkcudbright) also offers points of comparison with both Dundonald and Carrick (Fig 64). It was probably built after Archibald received the lordship of Galloway from David II in 1369, though whether before or after he inherited the earldom of Douglas in 1388 remains uncertain. There was also a later Stewart connection resulting from the marriage of Margaret Stewart, the eldest daughter of Robert III, to Archibald's son, Archibald, 4th earl of Douglas. Margaret continued to live at Threave after her husband's death in 1424. The tower measures 18.6m north–south by 12.2m east–west, with walls some 2m thick, and stands 22.5m high. The entrance at first-floor level opens into a barrel-vaulted space separated by a timber floor from a basement, to which, as at Carrick, there was apparently no internal access unless by a timber stair. The first floor was divided into an entrance hall and a kitchen. From the north-west corner, a turnpike stair

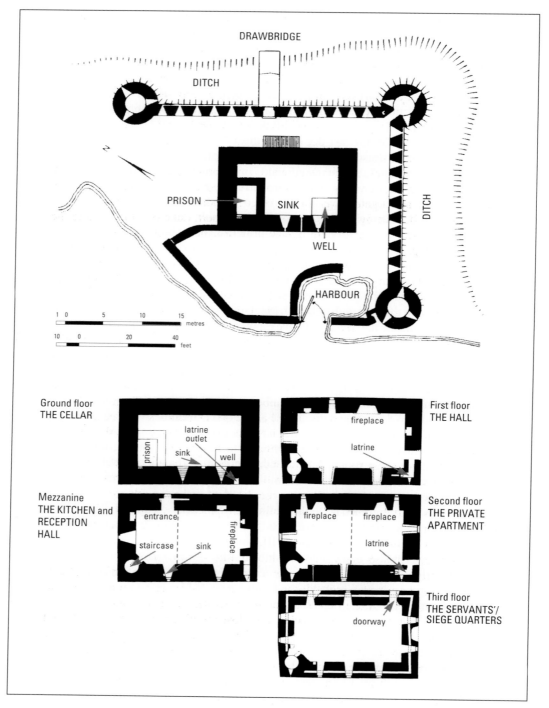

Fig 64 Threave castle plans (© Crown copyright, reproduced courtesy of Historic Scotland).

leads up to the hall above the barrel vault. This had a timber ceiling, a fireplace in the E wall, and a latrine closet behind the high table at the S end. From this level the turnpike continues up to two chambers on the third floor, each with a fireplace and the southern one provided with a latrine closet. Above this there was a very low entresol below the roof or garret, lit by a series of low windows, the purpose of which seems to have been to provide temporary accommodation, in time of need, for the defenders of the wall-head and of the permanent timber hoarding that surrounded the top of the tower (MacGibbon and Ross 1887–92, I, 157–67; RCAHMS 1914, 28–34; Cruden 1981, 115–18, pl. 17; Good and Tabraham 1981; Tabraham 1983; 1993).

A principal difference between the tower at Dundonald and those of Carrick and Threave was the pend that ran through its basement, making it a cross between a tower-house and a gate-tower. In this respect its direct descendant was Doune Castle (Fig 65), built by Robert II's third son, Robert, duke of Albany. Here the tower-house, standing at the NE corner of a roughly quadrangular enclosure, contains the principal gate to the castle; but it is not particularly defensible. Although the pend is vaulted and flanked by a porter's lodge and storage cellar, the gate is defended by no more than an iron yett, a slit machicolation (not a portcullis, as is sometimes claimed), and a box-machicolation at the wall-head. A stone stair from within the courtyard leads up to the lower hall, situated on the first floor. As at Dundonald this is covered by a plain barrel-vault, and is also provided with a double fireplace behind the dais at its E end. Unlike Dundonald, at Doune a chamber block or jamb was provided from the start. It is rounded in plan and projects from the E end of the N wall, giving some flanking cover to the gate. A turnpike stair in the north-eastern corner of the hall gives access to a vertical sequence of chambers within it, each provided with a fireplace and access to a corbelled latrine, as well as to the upper hall, above the barrel-vault. The upper hall was also heated by a finely decorated fireplace in its E wall; and on the south an alcove contained an oratory, separate from the hall by a timber partition. From this hall the main staircase in the NE corner continued up to a series of chambers and wall-closets on the third floor and the wall-head and garret above; another turnpike in the north-western corner also descended to the lower hall and its gallery (MacGibbon and Ross 1887–92, I, 418–29; Pringle 1987; Simpson 1938; 1982). Doune, however, was not to be the final word in royal tower gatehouses, for James IV began building another containing a hall and chambers at Rothesay Castle in 1512 (Dunbar 1999, 97–8; Pringle 1998, 157–8, 160–3).

At Doune, in addition to the tower containing the gate, there is also to the W an adjoining great hall, with a kitchen contained in a separate tower at the far end of it. The hall and kitchen takes up the north-western corner of a quadrangular enclosure, that was evidently intended to enclose building ranges on the W, S, and possibly the E. Although the external windows for these were built at the same time as the battlemented curtain wall and although tusking on the kitchen tower indicates where the W range was to be bonded on to it, these additional ranges were never built. The design of Doune is more mature than Dundonald and the castle shows clear evidence of having been built to a predetermined plan. The inner court and outer barmkin at Dundonald may yet have provided a model, albeit one more modest in scale and more constrained by the structures already existing on the site. The development of Dundonald's barmkin buildings, however, appears

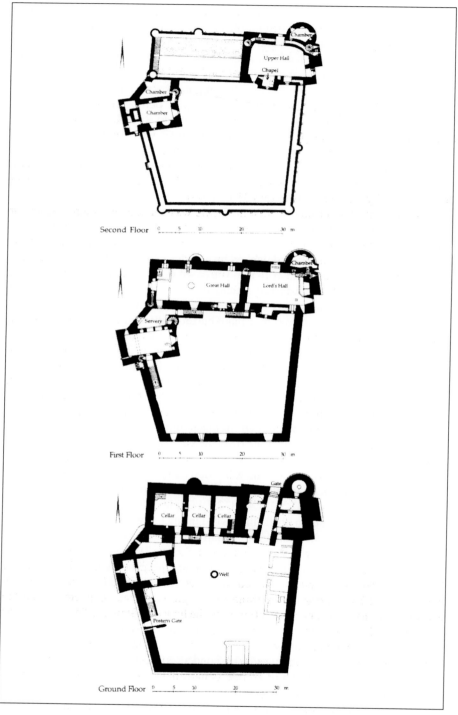

Fig 65 Doune Castle: plans (© Crown copyright, reproduced courtesy of Historic Scotland).

FANTASTIC SOFTWARE OFFER!

to have been more haphazard and their functions more utilitarian, including stabling for horses, a smiddy, and possibly accommodation for servants and stable-hands.

Periods 7–10 (c. 1449/50–present)

The history of the castle after the mid 15th century was one of gradual decline. From 1449/50 the keeper was Gilbert Kennedy, bailiff of the earldom of Carrick; and from 1448/9 the keepership and barony lands were in the hands of the Wallaces of Craigie. In 1526, William Wallace was granted feu of the lands, including the castle. Although the Wallaces held Dundonald until 1632, when they sold it to James Mathieson, it seems that by the 1590s they had already moved house to nearby Auchans Castle (NS 3548 3460).

It is difficult to tell exactly when the castle was abandoned as a residence, or the stages by which its buildings fell into dereliction (Fig 66). The subdivision of the upper hall inside the tower-house and the insertion of a second fireplace in its E wall suggest that it may still have been occupied in the mid 16th century or later; and a barony court was probably still functioning in the castle, perhaps in the lower hall, in the early 17th century, when we hear of people being locked up in the castle.

Dundonald seems to have declined as Auchans House grew (Fig 67), a process which took place gradually over several phases from c. 1545 until 1644 (MacGibbon and Ross 1887–92, II, 174–9; Zeune 1992, 139–10, figs 86–7). During this time it was not only the owners who moved to the new site; for examination of the masonry at Auchans suggests that it incorporates much material derived from the older castle. Wholesale demolition at Dundonald may therefore have begun by the later 16th century, when building work at Auchans seems to have been well underway. The slighter barmkin buildings were probably the first to be demolished and robbed of their stone, followed perhaps by the barmkin wall itself. The fact that the tower-house is still largely intact today suggests that it was never subject to deliberate quarrying, though James Boswell noted in 1773 that it had long been unroofed (Fig 68).

Conclusions

The significance of the recent programme of excavations can be summarised as having confirmed much of the scholarly opinion proffered since the architects MacGibbon and Ross first interpreted the ruins in the late 19th century. In many ways, the site has reflected everything that might have been expected given the etymology of its name and association with the house of Stewart. The excavations have enabled the synthesis of wide-ranging research on the nature of lordly settlement in the area through the identification of a series of fortified residences. Indications for the transition of each phase to its successor – hillfort, dun, vitrified timber-laced rampart, motte, timber hall, enclosure castle, and finally tower-house – were all revealed.

The result of the conservation works and archaeological investigations can now be appreciated on site (Fig 69), where there is a vistor centre which tells the story of the castle and houses finds from the excavation (Fig 70).

Fig 66 Engraving showing tinkers' camp in the ruins of Dundonald Castle at sunset, looking W with Auchans Castle behind (© Crown copyright, reproduced by courtesy of RCAHMS).

Fig 67 Sketch and plans of Auchans Castle (MacGibbon and Ross 1887–92, vol. 2, 175).

Fig 68 Photograph of castle taken by Valentine of Dundee from SE in 1880 (© Crown copyright, reproduced courtesy RCAHMS).

Fig 69 View of castle from the west showing the results of the conservation programme
(© Crown copyright, reproduced courtesy of Historic Scotland).

Fig 70 Dundonald Visitor's Centre opened in 2003 (© Crown copyright reproduced
courtesy of Historic Scotland).

References

Abbreviations

CDS = *Calendar of Documents Relating to Scotland Preserved in Her Majesty's Public Record Office*, J. Bain (ed.), 1881–88, London.

DGNHAS = Dumfriesshire and Galloway Natural History and Archaeological Society.

DES = *Discovery and Excavation in Scotland*, Council for Scottish Archaeology, Edinburgh.

ER = *Rotuli Scaccarii Regum Scotorum: The Exchequer Rolls of Scotland*, J. Stuart *et al.* (eds), 1878–1908. Edinburgh.

MW, I = *Accounts of the Master of Works for Building and Repairing Royal Palaces and Castles*, vol. I, H. M. Paton (ed.), 1957, Edinburgh.

NAS = National Archives of Scotland.

NMRS = National Monuments Record for Scotland.

RCAHMS = Royal Commision on the Ancient and Historical Monuments of Scotland.

RCAHMW = The Royal Commission on the Ancient and Historical Monuments of Wales

RMS = *Registrum Magni Sigilli Scotorum: The Register of the Great Seal of Scotland, 1306–1668*, 12 vols, J. B. Paul and J. M. Thomson (eds), 1984, Edinburgh

RRS = *Registrum Regum Scotorum*, 8 vols, G. W. S. Barrow *et al.* (eds), 1960– , Edinburgh.

Aitken, M. J. 1983 Dose Rate Data in SI Units, *PACT* 9, 69–76.

Aitken, M. J. 1998 *An introduction to optical dating: the dating of Quaternary sediments by the use of photon-stimulat*, Oxford.

Alcock, L. 2003 *Kings & Warrior Craftsmen & Priests*, Edinburgh.

Alcock, L. and E. A. Alcock 1987 Reconnaissance Excavations on Early Historic Fortifications and Other Royal Sites in Scotland, 1974–84: 2 Excavations at Dunollie Castle, Oban, Argyll. *Proc. Soc. Antiq. Scot.* 117, 119–47.

Alcock, L. and E. A. Alcock 1990 Reconnaissance Excavations on Early Historic Fortifications and Other Royal Sites in Scotland, 1974–84, Excavations at Alt Clut, Clyde Rock, Strathclyde, 1974–75, *Proc. Soc. Antiq. Scot.* 120, 95–149.

Alcock, L. and E. A. Alcock 1992. Reconnaissance Excavations on Early Historic Fortifications and Other Royal Sites in Scotland 1974–84: 5A – Excavation and Other Fieldwork at Forteviot, Perthshire, 1981. B – Excavations at Dunnottar, Kincardineshire, 1984, *Proc. Soc. Antiq. Scot.* 122, 215–87.

Alcock, L. *et al.* 1989 Reconnaissance Excavations on Early Historic Fortifications and Other Royal Sites in Scotland 1974–84: 3 Dundurn, *Proc. Soc. Antiq. Scot.* 119, 189–226.

Allason-Jones, L. and D. M. Jones 1994 Jet and Other Materials in Roman

Artefact Studies, *Archaeologica Aeliana*, 5s., 22, 265–72.

Allason-Jones, L. and R. Miket 1984 *The Catalogue of Small Finds from the South Shields Roman Fort*, Newcastle.

Anderson, A. O. 1908 *Scottish Annals from English Chroniclers A.D. 500 to 1286*, 2 vols, reprinted 1991, Stamford.

Anderson, A. O. 1922 *Early Sources of Scottish History, A.D. 500 to 1286*, 2 vols, reprinted 1990, Stamford.

Anderson, J. 1900 Description of a collection of objects found in excavations at St Blane's, Bute, *Proc. Soc. Antiq. Scot.* 34, 307–25.

Apted, M. R. 1963 Excavation at Kildrummy Castle, Aberdeenshire, 1952–62, *Proc. Soc. Antiq. Scot.* 96, 208–36.

Amours, F. J. (ed.) 1903–14 *The Original Chronicle of Andrew of Wyntoun*, Scottish Text Society, Edinburgh.

Avent, R. 1989 *Criccieth Castle*. Cardiff.

Barrow, G. W. S. 1976 *Robert Bruce and the Community of the Realm*, Edinburgh.

Barrow, G. W. S. 1980 *The Anglo-Norman Era in Scottish History*, Oxford.

Barrow, G. W. S. 1989 The Tribes of North Britain Revisited, *Proc. Soc. Antiq. Scot.* 119, 161–4.

Barrow, G. W. S. 2004 *Saint Ninian and Pictomania*, 12th Whithorn Lecture, Whithorn.

Barrow, G. W. S. and A. Royan. 1985 James Fifth Stewart of Scotland, 1260(?)–1309, in K. J. Stringer (ed.), *Essays on the Nobility of Medieval Scotland*, Edinburgh, 166–190.

Bartlett, R. (ed. and transl.) 2002 *Geoffrey of Burton: Life and Miracles of St Modwenna*. Oxford.

Bede. *Ecclesiastical History of the English People*, ed. B. Colgrave and R. A. B. Mynors, Oxford, 1969.

Binford, L. 1981 *Bones, Ancient Men and Modern Myths*, New York.

Bond, J. M. 1994 The Faunal and Botanical Remains, in R. Luff and P. Rowley-Conwy (eds), *Whither Environmental Archaeology?*, Oxford, 128–32.

Boswell, J. 1786 *The Journal of a Tour to the Hebrides with Samuel Johnson LL.D.*, P. Levi (ed.), London, 1984.

Boyd, W. 1988 Cereals in Scottish Antiquity. *Circaea*, 5(2), 101–10.

Breeze, A. 2002 Brittonic place-names from south-west Scotland: Part 3 Vindogara, Elvan Water, 'Mondedamdereg', Troquhain and Tarelgin, *Trans. Dumfries Galloway Nat. Hist. Antiq. Soc.* 76, 107–12.

Brooks, C. M. 1980 Medieval Pottery from the Kiln Site at Colsoun, E Lothian, *Proc. Soc. Antiq. Scot.* 110 (1978–80), 379–82.

Broun, D. 2004 The Welsh identity of the kingdom of Strathclyde c. 900–c. 1200, *Innes Review* 55, 111–80.

Brown, R. A. 1976 *English Castles*, 3rd edition. London.

Brown, R. A., H. M. Colvin and A. J. Taylor 1963 *The History of the King's Works*, I–II, *The Middle Ages*. London.

Caldwell, D. H. and V. E. Dean 1992 The Pottery Industry at Throsk, Stirlingshire, in the 17th and early 18th century, *Post-Med. Archaeol.* 26, 1–46.

Caldwell, D. H., G. Ewart and J. Triscott 1998 Auldhill, Portencross. *Archaeol. J.* 155, 22–81.

Callander, J. G. 1927 A Symbol Stone from Fiscavaig, Skye; and Early Iron Age hoard from Crichie, Aberdeenshire; and Cinerary Urns from Seamill, West Kilbride, Ayrshire, *Proc. Soc. Antiq. Scot.* 61 (1926–7), 241–51.

Campbell, E. 1996 The Archaeological Evidence for Contacts: Imports, Trade and Economy in Celtic Britain AD 400–800, in K. R. Dark (ed.), *External Contacts and the Economy of Late Roman and Post-Roman Britain*, Woodbridge, 83–96.

Campbell, E. 1997 The Early Medieval Imports, in Hill 1997, 297–322.

Campbell, E. forthcoming *Contintental and Mediterranean Imports to Atlantic Britain and Ireland, AD 400–800.*

Carter, S. P. and T. G. Holden 2000 Interpreting Prehistoric Cultivation using the Combined Evidence of Plant Remains and Soils: An Example from Northern Scotland, in J. P. Huntley and S. Stallibrass (eds), *Taphonomy and Interpretation*, Oxford, 1–12.

Châtelain, A. 1988 *Evolution des châteaux forts dans la France au moyen âge*, Strasbourg.

Childe, V. G. 1941 Examination of a Prehistoric Fort on Cairngryfe Hill, near Lanark, *Proc. Soc. Antiq. Scot.* 75 (1940–41), 213–8.

Clancy, T. O. 1998 *The Triumph Tree Scotland's Earliest Poetry AD 550–1350*, Edinburgh.

Clancy, T. O. 2001 The real St Ninian, *Innes Review* 52I, 1–28

Clancy, T. O. forthcoming Ystrad Clud (Strathclyde), in J. Koch (ed.), *Encyclopaedia of Celtic Culture*, Boston, Mass.

Close-Brooks, J. 1986 Excavations at Clatchard Craig, Fife, *Proc. Soc. Antiq. Scot.* 116, 117–84.

Coldstream, N. 2003 Architects, Advisors and Design at Edward I's Castles in Wales, *Architectural Hist.* 46, 19–36.

Cowan, I. and D. E. Easson. 1976 *Medieval Religious Houses: Scotland*, London and New York.

Cowie, T. 1978 Carwinning Hill, Hillfort, Cairn, Structural Remains, *Discovery and Excavation in Scotland*, 28.

Craig, D. 1994 The Early Medieval Sculpture of the Glasgow Area, in A. Ritchie (ed.), *Govan and its Early Medieval Sculpture*, Stroud, 73–91.

Creighton, O. H. 2002 *Castles and Landscapes*, London and New York.

Crone, A. 2000 *The History of a Scottish Lowland Crannog: Excavations at Buiston, Ayrshire 1989–90*, Edinburgh.

Cruden, S. H. 1981 *The Scottish Castle*, 3rd edn, Edinburgh.

Curle, A. O. and J. E. Cree. 1921 Account of the Excavations on Traprain Law during the Summer of 1920, *Proc. Soc. Antiq. Scot.* 55 (1920–21), 153–206.

Davis, M. 1993 The Identification of Various Jet and Jet-like Materials Used in the Early Bronze Age in Scotland, *The Conservator* 17, 11–18.

Dillon, W. 1966 Three Ayrshire Charters, *Ayr Archaeol. Nat. Hist. Coll.* 7, 28–38.

Driscoll, S. T. 1998 Church Archaeology in Glasgow and the Kingdom of Strathclyde, *Innes Review* 49, 94–114.

Driscoll, S. T. 2002 *Alba the Gaelic Kingdom of Scotland AD 800–1124*, Edinburgh.

Driscoll, S. T. 2003 Govan: an early Medieval Royal Centre on the Clyde, in

R. Welander, D. Breeze and T. O. Clancy (eds), *The Stone of Destiny Artefact and Icon*, Edinburgh 77–84.

Driscoll, S. T. 2004 The Archaeological Context of Assembly in Early Medieval Scotland – Scone and its Comparanda, in A. Pantos and S. Semple (eds), *Early Medieval Assembly Places*, Dublin, 73–94.

Driscoll, S. T., O. O'Grady and K. Forsyth 2005 The Govan School Revisited; Searching for Meaning in the Early Medieval Sculpture of Strathclyde, in S. Foster and M. Cross (eds), *Able Minds and Practised Hands*, Society for Medieval Archaeology Monograph, Leeds, 135–58.

Driscoll, S. T. and P. A. Yeoman. 1997 *Excavations within Edinburgh Castle in 1988–91*, Society of Antiquaries of Scotland, Monograph Series 13, Edinburgh.

Dunbar, J. G. 1999 *Scottish Royal Palaces: The Architecture of the Royal Residences during the Late Medieval and Early Renaissance Periods*, East Linton.

Duncan, A. A. M. 1975 *Scotland: The Making of the Kingdom*, Edinburgh.

Edwards, L. 1988 Seventeenth and Eighteenth Century Tyneside Tobacco Pipe Makers and Tobacconists, in P. Davey (ed.), *The Archaeology of the Clay Tobacco Pipe, XI*, BAR Brit. Ser., 192, Oxford, 1–164.

Ewart, G. 1985 *Cruggleton Castle: Report of Excavations 1978–1981*, DGNHAS monograph series, Dumfries.

Ewart, G. 1994 Dundonald Castle – Recent Work, *Château-Gaillard* 16, 167–78.

Fairwether, A. D. and I. B. M. Ralston 1993 The Neolithic Hall at Balbridie, Grampian Region, Scotland: The Building, the Date and Plant Macrofossils, *Antiquity* 67, 313–23.

Fawcett, R. 1994 *Scottish Architecture from the Accession of the Stewarts to the Reformation, 1371–1560*, Edinburgh.

Fawcett, R. 2002 *Scottish Medieval Churches: Architecture and Furnishings*, Stroud.

Fleury, M. and V. Kruta 2000 *Guide et monographie: le château du Louvre*, Dijon.

Forsyth, K. 2000 Evidence of a Lost Pictish Source in the *Historia Regnum Anglorum* of Symeon of Durham, in S. Taylor (ed.), *Kings, Clerics and Chronicles in Scotland, 500–1297*, Dublin, 19–34.

Gardelles, J. 1986 De Saint Louis à Philippe le Bel: le xiiie siècle, in J.-P. Babelon, *Le château en France*, Paris, 79–93.

Gillespie, J. H. 1939 *Dundonald – A Contribution to Parochial History*, 2 vols, Glasgow.

Good, G. L. and C. J. Tabraham 1981 Excavations at Threave Castle, Galloway, *Med. Archaeol.* 25, 90–140.

Goodall, J. 2000 Dover Castle and the Great Siege of 1216, *Château-Gaillard* 19, 91–102.

Gray, H. StG. and A. Bulleid 1953 *The Meare Lake Village*, II, Taunton Castle (privately printed).

Greig, R. A. 1991 The British Isles, in W. van Zeist, K. Wasylikowa and K. Behre (eds), *Progress in Old World Palaeoethnobotany*, Rotterdam, 299–334.

Guido, M. 1978 *The Glass Beads of the Prehistoric and Roman Period in Britain and Ireland*, London.

Guido, M. 1999 *The Glass Beads of Anglo-Saxon England*, London.

Hall, S. and J. Haywood (eds) 2001 *The Penguin Atlas of British and Irish History*, London.

Hamilton, J. R. C. 1956 *Excavations at Jarlshof, Shetland*, Edinburgh.

Hay Fleming, D. 1909 Notice of a Sculptured Cross-shaft and Sculptured Slabs Recovered from the Base of St Andrews Cathedral by Direction of Mr Oldreive of HM Office of Works, with Notes of Other Sculptured Slabs at St Andrews, *Proc. Soc. Antiq. Scot.* 43 (1908–9), 385–414.

Hill, P. 1979 *Broxmouth Hillfort Excavations, 1977–1978: An Interim Report*. University of Edinburgh Occasional Papers, 2, Edinburgh.

Hill, P. 1982 Broxmouth Hill-Fort Excavations, 1977–8, in D. W. Harding (ed.), *Later Prehistoric Settlement in South-East Scotland*, University of Edinburgh Occasional Papers, 8, Edinburgh, 141–88.

Hill, P. 1997 *Whithorn and St Ninian: The Excavation of a Monastic Town, 1984–91*, Stroud.

Hillman, G. 1981 Reconstructing Crop Husbandry Practices from Charred Remains of Crops, in R. Mercer (ed.), *Farming Practice in British Prehistory*, Edinburgh, 123–162.

Hinton, P. 1990 Weed Associates of Recently Grown *Avena strigosa Scheber*, from Shetland, Scotland, *Circaea*, 8(1), 49–54.

Hunter, F. 1998 Cannel Coal, in D. H. Caldwell, G. Ewart and J. Triscott, Auldhill, Portencross, *Archaeol. J.* 155, 42–53.

Hunter, F., J. G. McDonnell, A. M. Pollard, C. R. Morris, C. C. Rowlands 1993 The Scientific Identification of Archaeological Jet-like Artefacts, *Archaeometry* 35, 69–89.

Innes, C. (ed.) 1832 *Registrum Monasterii de Passelet*, Maitland Club, Glasgow.

Johns, C. N. 1970 *Criccieth Castle, Caernavonshire/Castell Criccieth, Sir Gaernavon*, London.

Johns, C. N. 1978 *Caerphilly Castle, Mid Glamorgan/Castell Caerffilli, Morgannwg Ganol*, Cardiff.

Jones, R. E., R. Will, G. Haggerty and D. Hall, in press, Sourcing Scottish White Gritty Ware, *Medieval Ceramics* 26.

Kenyon, J. R. 1990 *Medieval Fortifications*, Leicester and London.

King, D. J. C. 1988 *The Castle in England and Wales, an Interpretative History*, London.

King, D. J. C. and L. Alcock 1969 Ringworks of England and Wales, *Château-Gaillard* 3, 90–127.

Kirby, D. 1962 Strathclyde and Cumbria: a survey of historical developments to 1093, *Trans Cumberland Westmoreland Archaeol. Antiq. Soc.* 72, 77–94.

Knight, J. 2000 *The Three Castles: Grosmont Castle, Skenfrith Castle, White Castle. Hen Gwrt Medieval Moated Site*, Cardiff.

Koch, J. 1997 *The Gododdin of Aneirin: Text and Context from Dark-Age North Britain*, Cardiff.

Laing, D. (ed.) 1879 *The Orygynale Cronykil of Scotland by Andrew Wytoun*, Edinburgh.

Lane, A. and E. Campbell 2000 *Dunadd: An Early Dalriadic Capital*, Oxford.

Leask, H. G. 1946 *Irish Castles and Castellated Houses*, Dundalk (repr. 1986).

Lewis, J. 2003 Excavations at Crookston Castle, Glasgow 1973–75, *Scott Archaeol J.* 25.1, 27–56

Lloyd, J. D. K. and J. K. Knight 1973 *Montgomery Castle, Montgomeryshire/ Castell Trefaldwyn, Sir Drefaldwyn*, London.

London Museum 1954 *Medieval Catalogue*, London (repr. 1967).

McCormick, F. 1992 Early Faunal Evidence for Dairying, *Oxford J. Archaeol.* 11, 201–9.

McDonald, R. A. 1997 *The Kingdom of the Isles: Scotland's Western Seaboard, c. 1100–c. 1336*, SHR Monographs, 4, East Linton.

MacGibbon, D. and T. Ross 1887–92 *The Castellated and Domestic Architecture of Scotland*, 5 vols, Edinburgh.

Macguire, D. M. 2000 Crookston Castle, Glasgow City (Paisley Parish), Medieval Castle, *Discovery and Excavation in Scotland*, 43.

MacIvor, I. 1993 *Edinburgh Castle*, London.

MacKie, E. 1976 The Vitrified Forts of Scotland, in D. Harding (ed.), *Hillforts: Later Prehistoric Earthworks in Britain and Ireland*, London, 205–35.

McNeill, T. E. 1981 *Carrickfergus Castle, County Antrim*, Northern Ireland Archaeological Monographs, I, Belfast.

McNeill, T. 1992 *English Heritage Book of Castles*, London.

McNeill, T. 1997 *Castles in Ireland: Feudal Power in a Gaelic World*, London and New York.

Macphaill, J. R. N. (ed.) 1914 *Highland Papers*, I, Scottish History Society, Edinburgh.

Macquarrie, A. 1990 Early Christian Govan: the historical context, *Records Scott. Church Hist. Soc.* 24, 1–17.

Macquarrie, A. 1997 *The Saints of Scotland: Essays in Scottish Church History AD 450–1093*, Edinburgh.

MacQueen, W. n.d. The Stewarts and Dundonald, unpublished paper.

Malden, J. (ed.) 2000 *The Monastery and Abbey of Paisley*, Paisley.

Mann, L. McL. 1925 Note on the Results of Excavations at Dunagoil, *Trans. Bute Nat. Hist. Soc.* 9, 56–60.

Martin, P. F. de C. 1987 Clay Pipes in the Rest of Scotland, in P. Davey (ed.), *The Archaeology of the Clay Tobacco Pipe*, X. *Scotland*, BAR Brit. Ser., 178, Oxford, 167–82.

Mesqui, J. 2001 *Château d'Angers*, Paris.

Munro, R. 1882, *Ancient Scottish Lake-Dwellings or Crannogs*, Edinburgh.

Nicholson, R. 1974 *Scotland: The Later Middle Ages*. Edinburgh History of Scotland, 2. Edinburgh.

Nisbet, H. 1996 Craigmarloch Hillfort, Kilmalcolm, in D. Alexander (ed.), *Prehistoric Renfrewshire*, Edinburgh, 43–58.

Oliphant, J. 1992 *Tonbridge Castle*, Tonbridge.

O'Neil, B. H. StJ. 1982 *Caerlaverock Castle*, Edinburgh.

Payne, S. 1973 Kill-off Patterns in Sheep and Goats, *Anatolian Studies* 23, 281–303.

Prescott, J. R. and L. G. Stephan 1982 Contribution of cosmic radiation to environmental dose, *PACT* 6, 17–25.

Pringle, D. 1987 *Doune Castle*, Edinburgh.

Pringle, D. 1995 *Rothesay Castle and St Mary's Church*, Edinburgh.

Pringle, D. 1998 Rothesay Castle and the Stewarts, *J. Brit. Archaeol. Assoc.* 151, 149–69.

Raftery, B. 1983 *A Catalogue of Irish Iron Age Antiquities*, Marburg.

Ralston, I. B. M. 1986 Yorkshire Television's Vitrified Wall Experiment at East Tullos, Aberdeen District, *Proc. Soc. Antiq. Scot.* 116, 17–40.

Ralston, I. B. M. 2004 *The Hill-Forts of Pictland since 'The Problem of the Picts'*, Groam House Lecture, Rosemarkie.

RCAHMS 1914 *Stewartry of Kirkcudbright*, Edinburgh.

RCAHMS 1992 *Argyll: An Inventory of the Ancient Monuments*, VII. *Mid Argyll and Cowal*, Edinburgh.

RCAHMW 2000 *An Inventory of the Ancient Monuments in Glamorgan*, III.1b. *Medieval Secular Monuments: The Later Castles, from 1217 to the Present*, Aberystwyth.

Ritchie, G. and A. Ritchie 1991 *Scotland, Archaeology and Early History*, Edinburgh.

Ritchie, G. and H. Welfare 1983 Excavations at Ardnave, Islay, *Proc. Soc. Antiq. Scot.* 113, 302–66.

Rivet, A. L. F. and C. Smith 1979 *The Place-names of Roman Britain*, London.

Roll, I. *et al.* 2000 Apollonia–Arsuf during the Crusader Period in the Light of New Discoveries, *Qadmoniot*, 33.1, 18–31 [in Hebrew].

Roll, I. and O. Tal 1999 *Apollonia–Arsuf: Final Report of the Excavations*, I. *The Persian and Hellenistic Periods*, Tel Aviv.

Ruckley, N. A. 1990 Water Supply of Medieval Castles in the United Kingdom, *Fortress* 7, 14–25.

Salch, Ch.-L. 1979 *Dictionnaire des châteaux et des fortifications du moyen âge en France*, Strasbourg.

Salch, Ch.-L. 1987 *Les plus beaux châteaux forts en France*, Strasbourg.

Sanderson, D. C. W. 1988a Thick source beta counting (TSBC): a rapid method for measuring beta dose-rates, *Nuclear Tracks and Radiation Measurements* 14, 203–8.

Sanderson, D. C. W. 1988b Fading of thermoluminescence in feldspars: characteristics and corrections, *Nuclear Tracks and Radiation Measurements* 14, 155–62.

Sanderson, D. C. W., F. Placido and J. O. Tate 1985 Scottish Vitrified Fort: Background and Potential for TL Dating, *Nucl. Tracts* 10, 799–809.

Sanderson, D. C. W., F. Placido and J. O. Tate 1988 Scottish Vitrified Forts: TL results from six study sites, *Nuclear Tracks and Radiation Measurements* 14, 307–16.

Simpson, W. D. 1924 The Excavation of Coull Castle, Aberdeenshire, *Proc. Soc. Antiq. Scot.* 58 (1923–4), 45–99, 370.

Simpson, W. D. 1935 The Castles of Dunnideer and Wardhouse in the Garioch, Aberdeenshire, *Proc. Soc. Antiq. Scot.* 69 (1934–5), 460–70.

Simpson, W. D. 1938 Doune Castle, *Proc. Soc. Antiq. Scot.* 72, 73–83.

Simpson, W. D. 1950 Dundonald Castle. *Ayr Archaeol. Nat. Hist. Soc. Coll.*, 2nd series, 1 (1947–9), 2–51.

Simpson. W. D. 1965 *Kildrummy and Glenbuchat Castles, Aberdeenshire*,

Edinburgh.

Simpson, W. D. 1978 *Bothwell Castle*, Edinburgh.

Simpson, W. D. 1982 *Doune Castle*, Derby.

Speth, J. D. 1989 Early Hominid Hunting and Scavenging: The Role of Meat as an Energy Source, *J. Human Ecology* 18, 329–43.

Spurgeon, C. J. [1975] *The Castle and Borough of Aberystwyth*, Aberystwyth.

Stell, G. 1986 Dundonald Castle, *Archaeol. J.* 143, 145.

Stevenson, J. (trans.) 1988 *Mediaeval Chronicles of Scotland: The Chronicle of Melrose (from 1135 to 1264) and the Chronicle of Holyrood (to 1163)*, Llanerch.

Stevenson, R. B. K. 1955 Pins and the Chronology of Brochs, *Proc. Prehist. Soc.* 21, 282–94.

Strickertson, K., D. C. W. Sanderson, F. Placido and J. O. Tate 1988 *The Thermoluminescence of Vitrified Forts: New Results under Review*, Oxford, 625–33.

Strickertsson, K., F. Placido and J. O. Tate 1988 Thermoluminescence dating of Scottish Vitrified Forts, *Nuclear Tracks and Radiation Measurements* 14, 317–20.

Tabraham C. J. [n.d.] *Official Guide: Dundonald Castle*, Edinburgh.

Tabraham, C. J. 1983 *Threave Castle*, Edinburgh.

Tabraham, C. J. 1986 *Kildrummy Castle,* Edinburgh.

Tabraham, C. J. 1990 *Scottish Castles and Fortifications,* Edinburgh.

Tabraham, C. J. 1993 *Threave Castle*, Edinburgh.

Tabraham, C. J. 1994 *Bothwell Castle*, Edinburgh.

Tabraham, C. J. 1997 *Scottish Castles*, Edinburgh.

Talbot, E. 1974 Early Scottish Castles of Earth and Timber – Recent Fieldwork and Excavation, *Scot. Archaeol. Forum* 6, 48–53.

Taylor, A. J. 1950 Master James of St. George, *Eng. Hist. Rev.* 65, 433–57.

Taylor, A. J. 1972 *Rhuddlan Castle, Flintshire*, Cardiff.

Taylor, A. J. 1980 *Beaumaris Castle/Castell Biwmares, Gwynedd*, Cardiff.

Taylor, A. J. 1984 Documents Concerning the King's Works at Linlithgow, 1302–3, in D. J. Breeze (ed.), *Studies in Scottish Antiquity Presented to Stewart Cruden*, Edinburgh, 197–95.

Taylor, A. J. 1988 *Harlech Castle*, Cardiff.

Taylor, S. 1998 Place-names and the Early Church in Scotland, *Records Scott. Church Hist. Soc.* 28, 1–22.

Thomas, C. 1959 Imported Pottery in Dark-Age Western Britain, *Med. Archaeol.* 3, 89–111.

Thoms, L. 1983 Appendix 2: Preliminary List of North European Pottery from Scotland, in P. Davey and R. Hodges (eds), *Ceramics and Trade*, Sheffield, 254–55.

Toy, S. 1954 *The Castles of Great Britain*, London.

Turner, R. 2002 *Chepstow Castle,* Cardiff.

van der Veen, M. 1985 Carbonised Plant Remains, in G. J. Barclay (ed.), Excavations at Upper Suisgill, Sutherland, *Proc. Soc. Antiq. Scot.* 115, 188–91.

Watt, D. E. R. (ed.) 1993–8 *Scotichronicon by Walter Bower*, 9 vols. Aberdeen.

Waterman, D. M. 1959 Excavations at Lismahon, Co. Down, *Med. Archaeol.* 3,

139–76.

Watson, F. 1998 *Under the Hammer: Edward I and Scotland, 1286–1306*, East Linton.

Watson, G. P. H. 1918 Notes on the Excavation of an Artificial Mound at Kidsneuk, Bogside, Parish of Irvine, Ayrshire, *Proc. Soc. Antiq. Scot.* 52 (1917–18), 60–70.

Watson, W. 1926 *The Celtic Place-names of Scotland*, Edinburgh.

Wilkinson, J. G. 2002 Deep thoughts on the Devon, and a fresh look at the Nith, *Nomina* 25, 139–45.

Williams, I. 1968 *The Poems of Taliesin*, Dublin.

Yeoman, P. A. 1995 *Medieval Scotland: An Archaeological Perspective*, London.

Yeoman, P. A. 1998 Excavations at Castle of Wardhouse, Aberdeenshire, *Proc. Soc. Antiq. Scot.* 128, 581–617.

Zeune, J. 1992 *The Last Scottish Castles*, Internationale Archaeologie, 12, Buch am Erlbach.